Family Days in the Countryside around Portsmouth and the South Downs

John and Veronica Price

G000135082

Wayahead Publishing

First Published 2001
a b c d e
ISBN 0-9540163-0-0

Maps are reproduced from the Ordnance Survey mapping on behalf of The Controller of Her Majesty's Stationery Office © Crown Copyright. MC 100021185

Pictures © John Price 2001, unless specifically credited.

Published by Wayahead Publishing, 27 Cheddar Close, Frome, Somerset BA11 2DT.
e-mail us at info@wayaheadpublishing.co.uk
visit our website at www.wayaheadpublishing.co.uk

Printed by Jensen Press (SW) Limited, Bofors Park, Artillery Road, Lufton Trading Estate, Yeovil, Somerset BA22 8YH.

While every effort has been made to ensure the accuracy of information in this book, the countryside is forever changing, and rights of way are often modified. The authors and the publishers cannot accept responsibility for errors or omissions, or for changes in details given. Similarly, although we have tried to identify possible safety risks on the routes, walkers and cyclists must consider themselves responsible for their own safety and for those in their charge.

In this book we undertake to run the Give-me-Five and Pubberstamping Competition, and to report updates to walks and rides via our web site, at least until the end of December 2003. We are a small partnership and should unforeseen circumstances befall one of us, we may have to discontinue these operations. This would only be done in serious circumstances.

Finally, if you find an inaccuracy in text or maps, please either:
log on to www.wayaheadpublishing.co.uk to check status and advise us if necessary, or write to us at the address above.

CONTENTS

PORTSMOUTH to 🚢

Bilbao	30 hrs
Caen	6 hrs
Cherbourg	5 hrs
Le Havre	6 hrs
St Malo	9 hrs

Scale: 1:250 000 or 1 inch to 4 miles (1cm to 2.5km)

INTRODUCTION

Over the past few years when we were bringing up a family in the Portsmouth area, we had some wonderful days in the summer months exploring the lovely countryside. From these experiences we have written this "countryside handbook" - a book that we invite you to use to explore the countryside around Portsmouth. Our aim has been to include the best walks and rides within about 30 miles of Portsmouth and Chichester, and we hope that you enjoy them as we did.

We have tried to cram this book full of all the information that you will need to enjoy your trips into the countryside. You can start your walks and rides from a pub if you wish and a fact file is provided on the facilities that each pub offers. The pubs have agreed to stamp this book as a record of your progress in completing the walks and rides, and there will be a prize for the first completed record received by us. If you wish to avoid pubs there is an alternative start point - usually a public car park.

We love to see children enjoying the countryside with their parents and we have thought hard about what we could include to provide interest for children as well as adults. We have included with each walk a Give-me-Five Treasure Hunt. This is a test of observation for children as they walk the route and we hope that this will reduce the incidence of "How much further is it now Dad?", that sometimes starts only a few steps after setting out. There are regular prizes for this as well - please see Page 14 for details. Also, with the family in mind, we have produced our Rainy Day Guide for those days when the weather is not so good. This is a selection of places when a walk or ride is not possible, but a family day still is.

The countryside is forever changing and as soon as this book is printed

Never too young to start! © Julia Bayne/Sustrans

changes will take place. That is why we have introduced an on-line information service. We hope that you will feel that this is your book as well as ours. We invite you to become involved by letting us know of any changes that you come across. We will then pass them on to everyone via our web site. Please refer to Page 7 for more about this exciting new development, and how to contact us.

Although we have assumed that this book will be used by people living in South East Hampshire and West Sussex, we also had tourists in mind when writing it. Although you may not be in the area long enough to enter the competitions, we would still like to hear from you. Have you found the book useful? How could future editions be improved? Our mission at Wayahead Publishing is to produce the very best local walking and cycling guide books. Have we succeeded or failed? Let us know - we would love to hear from you.

Well, that's enough waffling from us. Time spent reading this, is time wasted not enjoying this beautiful countryside of ours. We are confident that after using this book, you should feel fitter in mind, body and spirit. We wish you many hours of simple enjoyment in the countryside.

Happy Walking and Cycling!
John and Veronica Price

KEEPING YOUR BOOK UP TO DATE

You can help us ....

We want you to find this book thoroughly useful and reliable during its life and we also want to keep it up to date for you. That is where we can all work together. Although we have researched the book very thoroughly, a surprising amount of change occurs in the countryside over a comparatively short period - fingerposts fall over, stiles become rickety, trees blow down, field paths are ploughed up, and rights of way diverted. We have many years of experience of writing these guidebooks and during this time

Below:
Who moved the fence?

we have learnt to avoid referring to impermanent features wherever possible. We have also utilised Ordnance Survey mapping and this should help you to navigate if a navigation point - say a fingerpost - has been damaged. However, over a period of time changes will inevitably occur.

That is why we have provided an on-line information service that provides you with updates that have occurred since the book was published, so that you can start your walk safe in the knowledge that you will have the latest information. If you visit our web site at www.wayaheadpublishing.co.uk you will find a page that provides the latest information on the walks and rides in this book. We undertake to provide this service at least until the end of December 2003.

However, we rely on your help to keep our book up to date and we encourage you to feed back to us any problems that you find. So, if you believe that any of the walk or ride instructions need to be changed, then please contact us with a proposed amendment. If you have an internet connection, then it would be helpful if you could visit our web site first to see whether the problem has already been identified. When we have reviewed what you have proposed, we will place the result on our web site for the information of all our readers. Please see the foot of the page to find out how to contact us.

Please help us to help you!

How to contact us ....

To advise us of a proposed amendment, you can either:

- Visit our web site - www.wayaheadpublishing.co.uk and use the e-mail link to contact us, or
- Send an e-mail to john@wayaheadpublishing.co.uk, or
- Write to Route Information (P&SD), Wayahead Publishing, 27 Cheddar Close, Frome, Somerset, BA11 2DT.

RAINY DAY GUIDE

Sometimes we have really looked forward to a walk or a cycle ride at the weekend, only to find that the weather forecast that was so promising earlier in the week, turned out to be completely wrong. There is no doubt that your options are drastically reduced in wet weather and if you have a young family, it's often difficult to find somewhere to go that is both interesting and yet not too expensive. We have selected, in alphabetical order, 20 places that are worth visiting on a wet day. We have not accepted any payment for inclusion of these attractions - they are listed because we believe that as a set they offer something for each member of the family.

Amberley Museum: This is mid-way between Arundel and Storrington on the B2139. It is definitely suitable for a whole day out as there is so much to enjoy. Craftspeople are to be found using traditional materials and tools to produce a range of goods. As well as the regular activities there is also a programme of special events that cover most weekends from March to October. There is a café and a picnic area, should weather permit. All areas are accessible by wheelchair. Dogs are admitted if kept on a lead. Opening times are daily, except for Mondays and Tuesdays that are not at holiday times: 10am - 6pm from mid-March until the end of October. Tel: 01798 831370; Web: www.amberleymuseum.co.uk

The Bear Museum: Of all our treasured childhood posses- sions it is probably our teddy bear that we hold most dear. The curator of this entrancing museum, Judy Sparrow, started her collection in a charming 18th century house in Dragon Street, Petersfield, in 1981. The number of bears grew so quickly that by 1984 the museum, the first of its kind in Britain, was opened. Today, it is internationally known and the collection includes teddy bears of all ages and sizes. Opening times are Tuesday to Saturday inclusive: 10am - 5pm. Admission is free. Tel: 01730 265108; Web: www.bearmuseum.co.uk.

Bosham Walk: In the old-world setting of this craft centre (look for the sign of the fisherman in the village) you will also find a fascinating collection of little shops selling jewellery, chocolates, antiques, African Arte- facts, children's clothing, dried flowers and much more. The spacious art gallery holds work of local artists and those of national and international repute. The exhibitions are changed regularly and visiting craftspeople come to demonstrate and sell their work. After your browse, relax with a cup of fresh coffee and a home-made snack in the Coffee Shop. Opening times are daily: 10am - 5.30pm.

Chichester District Museum: The museum is housed in an 18th century corn store. Chichester has a fascinating history that goes back through Medieval, Saxon and Roman times. There are displays on the Civil War, Georgian, Victorian and 20th century life in Chichester. There are many 'hands on' activities, and events during the year like Fossil Hunting, Roman Day, Archaeological Activity days. Opening times are Tuesday to Saturday (all year round except for Public Holidays): 10am - 5.30pm. Admission is free. Tel: 01243 784683.

Chichester Guildhall Museum in Priory Park: This museum was originally built in 1269 as the church of the Greyfriars. In 1538, after the dissolution of the monasteries, the church became the town hall and later a courtroom. The poet William Blake was tried for sedition here in 1804. This part of the museum also holds special events like Heritage Days on specific days, but as a rule the museum is only open on Saturday afternoons, from midday to 4pm. Admission is free. Tel: 01243 784683.

Chichester Pallant House Gallery:
This is at 9, North Pallant, Chichester and is a lovely Queen Anne town house, built in 1713, with a peaceful walled garden. The rooms in the house have been carefully restored with period furnishings and fittings. The house also holds one of the largest collections of 20th century art in Britain. During the year other art exhibitions are also held here. The Gallery shop sells gifts and original work by local artists, designers and craftspeople. There is a café selling light refreshments. Opening times are Tuesday to Saturday: 10am - 5pm; Sundays and Bank Holidays: 12.30pm - 5pm. Tel: 01243 774557.

Chichester Victorian Hall of Music - Mechanical Music and Doll Collection: This museum, one mile east of Chichester in Church Road, Portfield, is a magical place for those interested in Victoriana or fascinated by mechanical music. A guided demonstration tour takes you around the 100-year-old collection of superb Victorian and Edwardian musical artefacts. Children will love the beautiful collection of Victorian and Edwardian dolls, and to please the boys, there is even a suit of armour! Opening times are Wednesdays: 1pm - 4pm during June, July, August and September. Tel: 01243 372646.

Fishbourne Roman Palace: This is situated just west of Chichester and signposted from the A27. The Roman foundations

and mosaic floors that were uncovered in 1960 proved to be one of the most exciting and important archaeological finds of the 20th century. The mosaic floors are now covered and protected by the museum building. The history of Fishbourne from its Roman beginnings to present times is created through displays, an audio-visual programme and archaeological remains found on the site. Parking is free. There is a cafeteria, souvenir shop and places to picnic outside. The museum has good facilities for disabled people. Opening times are daily from 10am, but closing times vary according to the time of year. Tel: 01243 785859; E-mail: adminfish@sussexpast.co.uk

Gilbert White's House and The Oates Museum: If you want to find out more about Gilbert White and his life and works (featured in Walk 12), then visit his charming 18th century home in the High Street, Selborne. A further museum of historic interest is The Oates Museum which is devoted to the remarkable Oates family, in particular, 'Titus' Oates, hero of Scott's ill-fated Antarctic expedition and Frank Oates, his Victorian uncle. Refreshments are available in the Tea Parlour. There is access to the ground floor for disabled visitors. Opening times are daily from 11am - 5pm, 1st January to 24th December. Tel: 01420 511275.

Intech - Interactive Technology Exhibition: If you want to do something that is challenging, stimulating and fun for all the family then come to this exhibition created by the Hampshire Technology Centre Trust in Romsey Road, Winchester. From Winchester, travel along the A3090 road to Romsey and look for Kings School, then take the first turning on the right. The 'hands-on' activities cover aspects of science, technology, design and engineering. Car parking is in the adjacent car park. Opening times are Monday to Sunday (includes most weekends): 10am - 4pm. Admission is free. Tel: 01962 863791.

Jane Austen's House: If you have
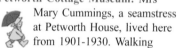
enjoyed reading Jane Austen's books or watching the dramatisations on film or television, then no doubt a visit to her house at Chawton, south of Alton, will be of great interest as many mementoes of her life and writings are to be found here. The house is a private museum and kept much the same as it was when she lived here. Outside the garden has been restored to its original state. Opening times vary according to the time of year. Tel: 01432 83262.

Petworth Cottage Museum: Mrs Mary Cummings, a seamstress at Petworth House, lived here from 1901-1930. Walking around the house you will feel as if you have stepped back in time and come to visit Mrs Cummings as a friend or neighbour. The kettle is on the hob, the table laid for tea and Mrs Cummings is in the sewing room surrounded by haberdashery and waiting work. Opening times are Wednesdays to Sundays (inclusive): 2pm - 4.30pm, April - October. Tel: 01798 342100.

The Royal Navy Submarine Museum at Gosport: For those fascinated by the history of submarine development and who would like to experience the 'feel' of life on board, then this is the museum to visit. The Museum is on Haslar Jetty Road. Displays and exhibits trace the history of the submarine from the age of Alexander the Great to the present day. Parking is free. There is a café, gift shop and places to picnic outside on the waterfront. Opening times are 10am - 4.30pm from November to March, and 10am - 5.30pm from April to October.

Tel: 023 9252; Web: www.rnsubmus.co.uk

Petworth Doll House Museum: This was started by Helen Zetter about 10 years ago. Here you will see an amazing collection of mainly modern doll houses by famous makers. The idea behind the enterprise is to give future generations an idea of how we live today. Using 2,000 miniature people, situations have been created in and around the houses to give the atmosphere of present day life. Opening times are Thursdays to Sundays: 10.30am - 5.30pm from March to October and Sundays: 11.30am - 4.30pm, during January and February. The Museum is closed in November and December. Tel: 01798 344044.

Stansted House: Follow the brown signs from the A3 at Rowlands Castle or from the A27 at Havant if you would like to see what life was like in an English country house in its Edwardian heyday. Stansted House is set in 1750 acres of beautiful park and woodland. The original house, built in 1688, was destroyed by fire in 1900 and a new building, exactly the same as the first, was built in 1903. There is a tea room, a childrens' play area and picnic areas if the weather permits. Opening times are Sundays to Wednesdays: 1pm - 5pm from 1st March to 31st October. Tel: 023 9241 2265; Web: www.stanstedpark.co.uk.

Tangmere Military Museum: Signposted from the A27 three miles east of Chichester, the museum opened in 1982 and tells the story of military flying in Tangmere from 1917 to 1970. During the Second World War the Royal Air Force at Tangmere played a vital part in the air war over Southern England. The Museum displays a poignant reminder of those times. The remains of aircraft, personal effects, photographs and paintings, tell their own story of the life and death struggle of those days. Parking is free. There is a cafeteria, a souvenir shop, places to picnic outside and facilities for the disabled. Opening times are daily: 10am - 4.30pm from February to November, and 10am - 5.30pm from March to October. Tel: 07971 580471.

Uppark: This prestigious National Trust property is to be found in South Harting near Petersfield on the B2146. Much of the late 17th century house was destroyed by fire in 1989; the story of this fire and the restoration is told in an award-winning multimedia exhibition. The property was re-opened in 1995, the house having been fully restored and the garden re-planted. There is a licensed restaurant and a kiosk for light refreshments. Near the car park is a picnic area should weather permit. There are good facilities for the disabled. Opening times are daily except Fridays and Saturdays. Although the house is only open from 1pm - 5pm, the gardens, exhibition, shop etc. are open from 11.30am. Tel: 01730 825415; Web: www.nationaltrust.org.uk/southern.

The Watercress Line: For 'Thomas The Tank Engine' enthusiasts a visit to this preserved heritage steam railway, near the A31 Winchester to Farnham road, is sure to be a great success. The line, which has been used in many film and tv productions, is 10 miles long and climbs through a series of deep cuttings, under and over bridges to reach the summit at Medstead and Four Marks Station. 'Days out with Thomas the Tank Engine and friends' are organised and you will need to telephone or visit the web site to find

details. Tel: 01962 733810; E-mail: watercressline@compuserve.com; Web: www.watercressline.co.uk

Weald and Downland Open Air Museum: This museum is just north of Chichester off the A286 Chichester to Haslemere road. There is so much of interest to be seen here that we feel sure that most families will be absorbed for a whole day, even if it is wet! Over 40 historic buildings from the region have been rescued from destruction. They were dismantled, brought here and carefully restored, and then re-built in their original form in this beautiful 50 acre setting. The Museum has an exciting programme of events and demonstrations of rural crafts. There is a café and a gift shop. Car parking is free and dogs are welcome if kept on a lead. Opening times are daily 10.30am - 6pm, 1st March to 31st October, and 10.30am on Wednesdays, Saturdays and Sundays between 1st Nov and 28th Feb.

Wickham Vineyard: If your family enjoy wine then a visit to this Hampshire vineyard, on the A32 north of Fareham, will enlighten you about this fascinating industry. Wickham wines have become renowned for their quality having won awards in both national and international competitions. If you visit in October you may see the harvest in full swing, and a visit in March may feature the bottling of wine of the previous vintage. Refreshments are available in The Terracotta Room with its marvellous views over the vineyard. Opening times are Monday to Saturday: 10.30am - 6pm; Sundays:11.30am - 5.30pm. Tel: 01329 834042.

PUBBERSTAMPING

This page is for the collectors amongst you. We have arranged for the pubs that are featured as the starting point for each walk or ride, to hold a "pubberstamp". When you have completed a walk or a ride, just ask the publican to stamp your book in the appropriate square, and you will have a record of completion.

We will award a *Family Days in the Countryside Sweatshirt* to the first completed record that we receive (please feel free to photocopy these pages). We will also award certificates to all completed records received up to at least 31st December 2003. You could of course use this book as a glorified pub guide and miss out the exercise bit altogether, but we know that the people who buy this book would not stoop to that sort of behaviour!

When you have completed all the walks and rides, just send in your entry with £2, and your name, address and telephone number to:

Pubberstamping Competition (P&SD), Wayahead Publishing, 27 Cheddar Close, Frome, Somerset, BA11 2DT.

Walk 1	Walk 2	Walk 3
Walk 4	Walk 5	Walk 6
Walk 7	Walk 8	Walk 9
Walk 10	Walk 11	Walk 12

Walk 13	Walk 14	Walk 15
Walk 16	Walk 17	Walk 18
Walk 19	Walk 20	Ride 1
Ride 2	Ride 3	Ride 4
Ride 5	Ride 6	Ride 7
Ride 8	Ride 9	Ride 10

GIVE-ME-FIVE COMPETITION

Making our walks fun for children ....

We want all members of your family to enjoy these walks in the countryside, and for this reason we have devised 20 simple treasure hunts for children. Our aim is to stimulate in children a love of walking, by developing their interest and knowledge of the

countryside, and the skills needed to be able to achieve this. Each treasure hunt is different and has five questions. The younger the child the more help they may need, but this is part of the fun of working together. Whether the clues are photographic, or are objects that need to be spotted, collected or drawn, they will all require observational skills. You may find particular topics interesting enough to investigate them further. If so, then visit the children's page on our web site and tell us about it (or alternatively write to us).

When at least 15 of the walks and treasure hunt questions are completed, we would like children to send their answers to us together with a picture drawn by them (no bigger than A4 size), entitled 'My Family in the Countryside'. Three times per year (at

the end of April, August and December) until at least 31st December 2003, we will judge the winning entry based on the most correct answers and best picture. The prize will be a certificate and a Family Days in the Countryside T-shirt. We will also post a selection of the best pictures on our childrens' web page. Entries are open to children who have not yet attained their thirteenth birthday. Send in your entry with name, age and address to:

Give-me-Five Competition (P&SD), Wayahead Publishing, 27 Cheddar Close, Frome, Somerset, BA11 2DT.

A WALK ON THE DOWNS ABOVE OWSLEBURY

(Where we start off with an old ship's timbers and also end up looking for ships)

Fact File..........

Starting Point: This walk starts from The Ship Inn.

Alternative Parking and Start Point: As an alternative, you can park at the public car park at Cheesefoot Head, and just complete the circular section. This will shorten the walk considerably but it will mean that you will not be able to complete the Give-me-5 Treasure Hunt.

Distance: Allow a little over 4 hours for this walk; the distance is 8.5 miles (13.7km).

Classification: 'Moderate' - This is a long walk with a single steady climb up to Cheesefoot Head.

Safety and Comfort: Special care should be taken at the crossing of the Corhampton/Winchester road by Bottom Pond Farm. This is a fast road and visibility is poor especially when returning to Owslebury. If you have children in your party make sure that they do not go ahead of you as they could be in the road before you realise. If you cross the A272 to Cheesefoot Head, this is also a fast road and great care should be taken here as well.

Maps: Ordnance Survey Landranger 1: 50 000 Series - Sheet 185.
Ordnance Survey Explorer 1: 25 000 Series - Sheet 132.
Ordnance Survey Pathfinder 1: 25 000 Series – Sheet 1264 (SU 42/52).
Map reference of start and finish - SU 512232.

Other Refreshment Possibilities: If you start from Owslebury, the Shearers is very close to the route at a distance of 1 and 8 miles (1.6 and 12.9 km).

Travel by Car: Owslebury lies about 8 mile (12.9km) south east of Winchester set back from the Corhampton/Winchester road.

Public Transport: Owslebury is served once a day from Winchester by Countywide Travel Bus Services 27B and 27C (Tel: 01256 465245). It is also served occasionally from Winchester and Bishops Waltham by Service 63 from the same company.

Background ....

If you are a stranger to Owslebury, you will not know how to pronounce the name of this village. It is certainly not pronounced as it is written - 'Owslebury'. We have heard it said with the first two syllables rhyming with bustle, but most Hampshire folk that we have met, and who have an opinion on the subject, seem to prefer a rhyme with 'jostle'. So, if you say 'Ostlebury', you will not go far wrong.

Sticking to the subject of this name for the moment, it would appear to have a rather peculiar meaning. According to Richard Coates in his book The Place-Names of Hampshire it is an Old English (Anglo-Saxon) word meaning 'blackbird fort'.

Although it is a hilltop village and

its physical situation may be responsible for the 'fort' part of the meaning, examination of local maps does not reveal any earth-works that could have given rise to the name.

The village itself sits comfortably on its hill, dominated by the church that stands high and looks across to Southampton. It could not be described as a picturesque village by any means, as it has houses of many styles - from terraced council-style homes to large and old timber-framed cottages. But this, and the football and cricket pitches you pass when entering the village, proves that the heart of Owslebury still beats and is not (like so many Hampshire villages), a place where only the very wealthy can live, and where you can sometimes feel unwelcome. It is not pretty enough to be found on the front of any picture-postcards as far as we are aware, but at least it has not lost its character and in fact you feel rather at home here.

You should note that this is the longest walk in the book, and we would recommend that you take a picnic and perhaps enjoy it near Cheesefoot Head.

The Walk ....

From The Ship Inn car park, turn right and continue along the lane with the

buttressed wall of Boyes Farm on the right and proceed down the steep hill. At the junction with Hensting Lane,

Give-me-Five Treasure Hunt

This is a hunt for the names of five homes around the route. Keep your eyes alert to spot them as you go. The initial letter of each one comprises the word "SHIPS". They do not occur in order.

The first is a home where a type of farm worker might live (S------- -------)

The second is where a prickly tree might grow (H---- -----)

The third is often associated with the second (I-- --- ----)

The fourth is usually a wet place (P--- -------)

The fifth is where an assertive male might stand (S---- ----)

turn right as directed to Owslebury and after about 300 yards (274 metres) take the left fork to avoid the route back to Owslebury; continue following the lane and after a further 300 yards (274 metres) or so you will come to a further junction by an isolated house - keep right here, avoiding the left turn.

Old signpost at Owslebury

At the junction, marked by a brick and flint house that is a mixture of old and new, carry almost straight on up the gravelled bridleway. This bridleway suddenly changes into a very wide and pleasant green track. It runs along the bottom of a shallow valley and crosses the busy Corhampton/Winchester road by a grey slate house (Bottom Pond Farm) where you should take great care. It then continues onward in a very pleasant fashion, cooly shaded in summer by a good selection of hazel, ash and crab apple trees many of which are covered in ivy.

The bridleway continues to follow the bottom of the shallow valley for a considerable distance. Turn left at the junction of bridleways (just before you pass under the power lines) and follow the bridleway uphill. You eventually emerge into more open countryside in a young plantation, to follow a roughly surfaced track. Pass from the track through the large blue double gates into a field and walk along the left edge of the field with a plantation on your left. Eventually you will walk across wide and open fields.

As you approach the busy A272, turn left away from another set of blue gates to take a bridleway that runs roughly parallel with the direction of the A272. (If however you want to visit Cheesefoot Head or return to the car park there, carry straight on and very carefully cross the A272).

The bridleway turns sharp right and continues through two wooden posts and then past a vertical white marker (a pipeline marker). At the next fingerpost that marks the crossing of bridleways, turn left and walk by the green gate and proceed gently downhill in a southwesterly direction through open fields into the distance.

You now walk for a mile on very open downland and then join a gravelly track with a small wooded area on the right. This area to the right of your route is part of Chilcomb

MOD range, and this land is out of bounds when the red flag is flying. However, the route that you are actually walking is a right of way at all times, although on some firing days you could possibly be held by a sentry until he has radioed through to ensure safe passage. The track becomes a surfaced lane by Hydes Cottages and you must follow this for 150 yards (137 metres). At this point take the bridleway off to the left. This is a very pleasant track, sunken in places and raised in others. It can be slightly overgrown, but remains reasonably walkable throughout most of the year.

You emerge briefly again at the busy Corhampton/ Winchester road before immediately turning away from it along the track as indicated by the public footpath waymarker, gradually diverging from the road. After just under half a mile, you will cross the track to Morestead Warren Farm - continue onward in approximately the same direction (ignore any possible turnings) and you will come to a point where the track swings sharply to the left. Here, leave the track by taking the footpath across the field that is indicated by a fingerpost. As you cross the field you will become aware of a small rectangular enclosure effectively forming an annex to the main field. At the far right corner of this you will find the stile.

You will discover that in fact there are two stiles which you should climb in succession and then bear slightly right across this field and you will soon see a stile in the corner. Climb this stile, turn right and if you started the walk from Owslebury, you will find yourself back on your original outward route. At the junction of bridleways turn right and walk to the point where you cross the Corhampton/Winchester road again - take great care here - please see the safety warning in the fact file. Carry on along the track until you come to

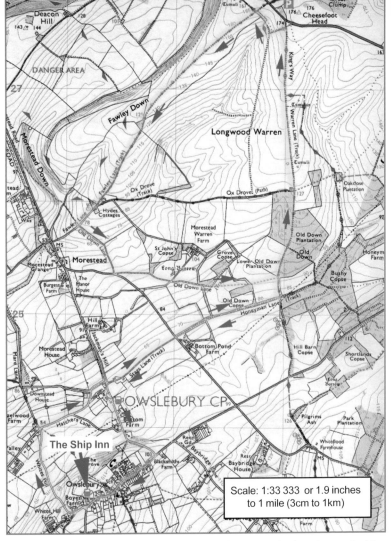

Scale: 1:33 333 or 1.9 inches to 1 mile (3cm to 1km)

the brick and flint house that is a mixture of old and new. Turn left and follow the lane up the hill to

Owslebury. At the junction marked by the very old signpost, turn right to walk the remaining 0.5 miles (0.8km) back to The Ship.

Pub File..........

The Ship Inn: Walkers are welcome and you can get your book 'pubberstamped' here. Opening times are 11am to 3pm and 6pm to 11pm on Mondays to Saturdays; midday to 10.30pm on Sundays. Bar food is available and there is a daily 'Specials' board as well as a wide range of good quality meals in the restaurant. Food is available daily from midday to 2pm and 6.30pm to 9.30pm. The pub serves real ale. Children are welcome and are allowed into at least one area of the premises. Dogs are permitted if kept on a lead. The licensee is happy for walkers to park their cars in the car park providing they patronise the pub before or after their walk. (Tel: 01962 777358).

TITCHFIELD HAVEN

(Where we see lots of birds and learn about a very old canal)

Fact File..........

Starting Point: This walk starts at the Queens Head in the High Street, Titchfield.

Alternative Parking and Start Point: There are two alternatives to parking at the pub. Very close to the pub is the short stay Barry's Meadow Car Park (entrance off Southampton Hill). This is free, but parking is limited at most times to 3 hours. A further alternative is an informal car park immediately by the canal at Bridge Street.

Distance: Allow 3 hours for the full walk, the distance is 6 miles (9.7km).

Classification: 'Gentle' - this is an extremely flat walk.

Safety and Comfort: If you are walking with children, you will need to supervise them carefully when walking the cliffs between Meon Shore and Sea House, as there is no fencing and there is a considerable drop to the beach.

Maps: Ordnance Survey Landranger 1: 50 000 Series - Sheet 196.
Ordnance Survey Explorer 1: 25 000 Series - Sheet 119.
Ordnance Survey Pathfinder 1: 25 000 Series - Sheet 1303 (SU 40/50).
Map reference of start and finish - SU 540049.

Other Refreshment Possibilities: The only places where food or drink can be obtained is in Titchfield - there are no opportunities along the route. There are at least three other pubs in Titchfield and tea rooms in South Street.

Travel by Car: Titchfield is situated alongside the A27 about 3 miles (4.8km) west of Fareham.

Public Transport: Titchfield is regularly served by First Provincial Bus Service No. 57 from Portsmouth and Warsash, No.72 from Gosport and Southampton and Nos. 79/80/80A from Fareham and Southampton (Tel: 01329 232208 or 023 92862412 for more information).

Background ....

This walk can readily be divided into three sections. The first section is a canal-side walk and takes you outside the western boundary of the Titchfield Haven Nature Reserve. The walk then leads you in a westerly direction along the shoreline. Finally, you return northwards to Titchfield through rather bleak and flat land used mainly for market gardening. The best part of the walk is the first section that follows the canal along the edge of the nature reserve from Titchfield to Meon Shore. If you have young children, you may wish to walk this section to the sea and return the same way. This will shorten the walk from 6 to 5 miles (9.7 to 8 km).

Titchfield Haven Nature Reserve is a very important site for wildlife and includes 309 acres (125 hectares) of wetland habitat, accommodating wintering wildfowl and waders in the

Doggy freedom, but keep your dog restrained when close to the reserve

Southeast England and the reserve is one of the strongholds for the species. If you walk the route in April or May, you should have a good chance of hearing this warbler in the lower stretches of the reserve, where the rushes are close-by on the left. We have often heard it at this point, but never seen one as it sings from a skulking position. Rather like the nightingale it is a case of "once heard never forgotten". With this bird it is the sheer volume of sound produced in its sudden explosive song that is so impressive. Along the edge of the haven, dog owners should keep their dogs under close restraint to avoid them straying into the reserve and possibly disturbing nesting birds. This walk may stimulate your interest in the reserve. You can visit from September 1st to March 25th, but you should obtain a permit first from the information centre at the reserve entrance close to Hill Head Harbour.

winter and rare nesting birds in the summer. Without doubt, one of the success stories of the reserve is the part it has played in the re-establish-ment of the Cetti's warbler since the 1960s. It is now relatively common in

The Titchfield Canal runs past the churchyard and water meadows almost to the sea. It is very old - we believe that it was the second artificial waterway ever to have been

Give-me-Five Treasure Hunt

The questions listed below can be answered simply by being observant as you walk through the village and the reserve - no prior knowledge is required and the questions are in order:

1. *When did Titchfield win the best kept village award?*
2. *Give an example of a wildfowl or wader that can be seen in the reserve.*
3. *Give an example of a bird that nests in summer.*
4. *Give an example of an orchid found in the reserve.*
5. *Give an example of a type of insect commonly found on the reserve.*

constructed in Britain. Before the canal, the River Meon presented a navigable channel from Titchfield to the sea and sizeable vessels used the village as a port. It is thought that the channel may have silted up and as a result the third Earl of Southampton built a dyke across the mouth of the river, and built the canal. Horse-drawn barges were used to transport goods between the sea lock and the village.

The Walk ....

Starting from the Queens Head, walk towards The Square, turn left into Church Street, and take the footpath around the right side of the church-yard. Cross the canal bridge and walk along the left (east) side of the canal. Cross the road, pass the car park and continue along the canal. From here, our route follows a course with the canal on the right for about 1½ miles (2.4km). Little description is therefore needed until the footpath meets the road at Meon Shore.

Cross straight across the road on its bend, and walk between the beach chalets and bungalows along the shingly path. By the last one, climb the stile to take the footpath up the incline to walk a narrow path along the cliff with gorse on the left. You then climb another stile to gain access to a slightly wider route and continue your way with scrub to the left and open fields to the right. When you get

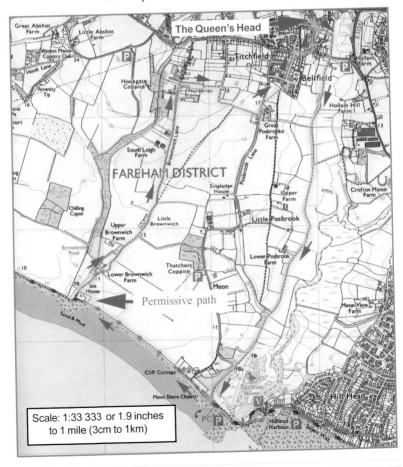

Scale: 1:33 333 or 1.9 inches to 1 mile (3cm to 1km)

Meon Shore

then emerge in a field, follow the edge of the field around to the triangulation point and then continue to the fingerpost. Here, take the gravelled track to walk in the direction of the three houses to the lane.

Turn left at the lane and walk for about 150 yards (137 metres) and then take the footpath off to the right by climbing the stile. Walk in the direction of the distant transmitting tower, climb the stile and walk down the hill to the road and turn left - this is Ransome Close. At the end of Ransome Close turn left for 20 yards (18 metres)and right into Lower Bellfield and down to the road where you turn right and back into Titchfield. At the Coach and Horses roundabout, turn into South Street to return to your starting point.

to a position where there is a large house (Sea House) looking out to sea you turn right to use the permissive path around the outside of the rear of the property. At the end, turn right to head north and the public footpath follows Sea House Drive.

At Lower Brownwich Farm you will meet a very wide six-bar metal gate and at this point you should swing right onto a concrete farm drive. You can either walk on the drive or use the footpath to its side. At the junction of concrete drives, avoid the right turn and continue straight on to Little Bronwich Farm. After about 100 yards (91 metres) you will come to some red houses and open barns on the left. This is wide open and windswept countryside with derelict market gardens and greenhouses with the glass blown in. Turn off right at the fingerpost sign. The enclosed path has laurel bushes on the left for about 200 yards (183 metres), then continues through a fairly narrow section with ivy covered trees on the right. You

Looking out for birds

Pub File.........

The Queens Head: Walkers are welcome and you can get your book 'pubberstamped' here. Opening times are 11am to 3pm and 6pm to 11pm on Mondays to Saturdays; midday to 3pm and 7pm to 10.30pm on Sundays. There is a restaurant, an extensive range of bar food and a daily 'Specials' board. Food is available daily from midday to 2pm and 7pm to 9pm, but no food is served on Sunday evenings. The pub serves real ale. Dogs are permitted if kept on a lead. The licensee is happy for walkers to park their cars in the car park providing they patronise the pub before or after their walk. (Tel: 01329 842154).

THE MEON VALLEY LINE

(And where we visit the village of many eating places)

Fact File..........

Starting Point: This walk starts from the King's Head at Wickham.

Alternative Parking and Start Point: It is possible to park in the village square. There is no charge but parking is limited to two hours - just about enough time to complete your walk. There is also a car park just off Mill Lane - see map for location.

Distance: Allow 2 hours for this walk, the distance is 4 miles (6.4km).

Classification: 'Gentle' - probably the flattest walk in the book.

Safety and Comfort: No problems.

Maps: Ordnance Survey Landranger 1: 50 000 Series - Sheet Sheet 196.

Ordnance Survey Explorer 1: 25 000 Series - Sheet 119.

Ordnance Survey Pathfinder 1: 25 000 Series - Sheet 1284 (SU 41/51).

Map reference of start and finish - SU 572114.

Other Refreshment Possibilities: There are many alternatives in Wickham. From tea rooms to brasseries, from pubs to bistros, the choice will amaze you.

Travel by Car: Wickham lies off the A32 Fareham to Alton road.

Public Transport: Wickham is extremely well-served by buses. First Provincial Service 38/38A runs from Fareham and Portsmouth and Service 138 from Fareham and Waterlooville (Tel: 023 92862412 or 01329 232208 for more information). Solent Blue Line Service 48C/D runs from Southsea and Winchester (Tel: 023 80618233). Stagecoach Hampshire Bus Service 69 runs from Southsea and Winchester (Tel: 01256 464501 for more information). This list is not exhaustive and only lists the main services.

Background ....

Wickham is a fine village with its large market square and its timbered cottages. It seems to have become a gastronomic centre in recent years as every time that we re-visit Wickham, yet another place to eat has appeared. It seems that almost every other shop is now either a pub, tearoom, brasserie or wine bar.

The early part of this walk follows the route of the old Meon Valley Railway. The line was opened in June 1903 and was operated by the London and South Western Railway Company. The permanent way was constructed

Chesapeake Mill

wide enough for two tracks, but only one was ever built. In the early days, the line was very busy and it carried more goods than passenger traffic, the main commodities being market garden produce (including strawberry trains in the summer), coal, milk and livestock. Closure of the line began in 1955 although some isolated sections carried on until 1968. The old line is a magnificent amenity for walkers and the usable section stretches for 11 miles (17.7 km) from Tapnage just

south-west of Wickham to West Meon. Its excellent access and straight aspect creates the possibility of circular walks or cycle rides that would not otherwise be possible. Another point of interest on this walk is Chesapeake Mill. This was rebuilt and renamed by John Prior who was a miller, using timber that he bought in 1820 from the American man-o'-war Chesapeake, a ship captured, as told by the ballad, by HMS SHANNON in the American War of Independence.

Give-me-Five Treasure Hunt

Shown below are five pictures around the route (not in order). Just keep alert and you will see the items as you walk. All you need to do is to tell us where they are by using the map to provide a 6-figure Ordnance Survey grid reference.

The Walk ....

With your back to the pub and looking out to the opposite side of the square, turn left and walk past the telephone box and then swing right by the White Lion. Continue down the road past the derelict Chesapeake Mill on the left, and over the River Meon. Immediately after passing under the railway bridge, turn right and gain access to the old Meon

Valley Line by climbing the steps. At the top, turn left to walk away from the bridge in a generally south westerly direction. You will pass over a river and a road bridge and a third (brick-built) bridge. Continue along this very pleasant old railway line at first through a golf course, and then you will be joined by a vineyard on your right. Continue to the end of the vineyard and then climb the high stile, turn right and walk up the left side of the vineyard for about 100 yards (91 metres). You will see a plank bridge and stile, which you should climb. You will then need to be bold here (if there are crops planted) and walk straight across this field.

At the opposite edge of the field, climb the stile and turn left onto the tarmac drive that follows the edge of the golf course. You will meet the road (Titchfield Lane), turn right here for about 90 yards (82 metres) until you are opposite Biddenfield Lane. Take the fingerposted footpath by the letterbox, which initially proceeds through a narrow wooded copse, you will be accompanied by garden panel fencing from time to time. You will

A Wickham cottage

View from the Meon Valley Line

eventually leave the copse to walk a route enclosed by fencing through smallholding land.

Climb a stile that takes you through an enclosure of ducks. Leave the ducks by the "dog-friendly" stile, cross the track to climb a further similar stile at which point you turn sharp left. After 35 yards (32 metres) turn right - you will have an ornamental pond away to your left at this point. Walk alongside the row of cupressus trees that screen the bungalow, swing left by a transformer, walk under a holly tree and continue with gorse bushes on your left. Descend a gorse-lined slope and cross the open field to enter the plantation of silver birches. After about 500 yards (457 metres) in this plantation you will pass over a small footbridge straddling a brook. A few steps after this you reach the edge of the plantation.

The correct route here was ploughed out at the time of walking. It heads across the field for about 200 yards (183 metres) and then turns right, back towards the wood that you have just left. The most sensible solution is to follow the track that

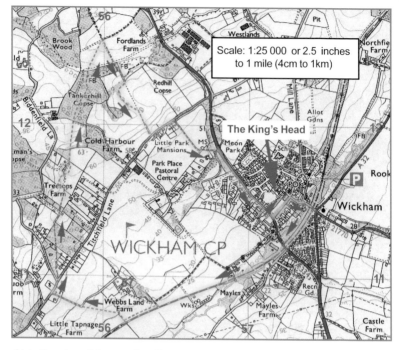

Scale: 1:25 000 or 2.5 inches to 1 mile (4cm to 1km)

skirts the edge of the wood until you see the small plastic yellow arrow and at this point turn right into the wood again. The wood is narrow at this point, you will walk a plank bridge. Keep walking in a constant (southerly) direction and you will soon reach the edge of the wood. Now at this point, you may find that the footpath has been ploughed, so you will need to be bold. Look up the hill to the large white houses lining the road. Walk in a direction generally toward the right-most house. At the time of walking, a small section of the path was not ploughed out and was tree-lined and overgrown as it approached the road at the top.

Meet the road and turn left, and take the first fingerposted path to the right, by a large red brick house. This path bisects a field that you leave by a kissing gate (the gate may be a few yards to the left of the apparent end of the path). Continue on for a few more steps, pass through a heavy iron gate, and you will emerge by the entrance to Park Place Pastoral Centre to meet the A334.

Turn right and walk the short distance back to the centre of Wickham and the King's Head.

Pub File..........

The King's Head: Walkers are welcome and you can get your book 'pubberstamped' here. Opening times are 10am to 11pm on Mondays to Saturdays; midday to 10.30pm on Sundays. There is a restaurant, an extensive range of bar food and a daily 'Specials' board. Food is available from midday to 2.30pm and 6pm to 9pm on Mondays to Saturdays; midday to 3pm on Sundays. The pub serves real ale. Children are welcome and are allowed into at least one area of the premises. Dogs are permitted if kept on a lead. Some overnight accommodation is available. Car parking is available in the vicinity. (Tel: 01329 832123).

A SHORT AND PLEASANT RAMBLE AROUND CHERITON

(Where we find a very watery place and also visit a famous battlefield)

Fact File..........

Starting Point: This walk starts from the Flower Pots pub in Cheriton.

Alternative Parking and Start Point: There are no car parks around the route, so if you are not parking at the Flower Pots, then we suggest that you park your car somewhere in Cheriton village. There are several places where the roads are suitable.

Distance: Allow 2 hours 15 minutes for this walk, the distance is 4.5 miles (7.2km).

Classification: 'Moderate' - One easy climb to gain access to the downs.

Safety and Comfort: No problems.

Maps: Ordnance Survey Landranger 1: 50 000 Series - Sheet 185.

Ordnance Survey Explorer 1: 25 000 Series - Sheet 132.

Ordnance Survey Pathfinder 1: 25 000 Series - Sheets 1264 (SU 42/52) and 1265 (SU 62/72).

Map reference of start and finish - SU 581283.

Other Refreshment Possibilities: There are no other opportunities on this walk for refreshment.

Travel by Car: Cheriton is situated on the B3046 just north of the A272 Petersfield to Winchester road.

Public Transport: Cheriton is served hourly on weekdays from Winchester and Petersfield by Stagecoach Hampshire Bus Service No. 67 (Tel: 01256 464501 for more information).

Background ....

Cheriton is a pretty and fairly quiet village once you have walked away from the main road. The source of the River Itchen is barely a mile away and it is a very watery place with streams everywhere, and large signs warning you of the likelihood of ducks crossing the road. The pretty river cannot seem to decide which course to take, as it divides up into several channels twisting this way and that, under bridges and around garden walls. There are not many villages in England where there are probably more ducks and geese than people, but we would guess this is the situation in Cheriton.

Aside from its ducks and geese,

The Flower Pots

Cheriton is also famous for an epic civil war battle. There is nothing to mark this fact anywhere as far as we can tell - except on Ordnance Survey maps. The battle took place east of the B3046 in the valley between Cheriton Wood and the village on 29th March 1644. If you walk these byways on a summer's day, nothing could be more peaceful than this gentle countryside. The land slopes gently down to the infant river and nothing noisier than a sheep or a skylark can be heard. But things were much different in the spring of 1644 when such a fierce battle took place that 2000 men were killed and buried in communal graves. Such was the intensity of the battle that the lanes on which the walk takes place were said to have run with blood. You can still see the burial mounds around the village. These lanes were a fundamental factor in the battle which ended with a Parliamentary victory and the Royalist forces retreating to Basing House.

On a more cheerful note, the name of the Flower Pots - the excellent pub that is our starting point - is worthy of some explanation. It all becomes clear when you discover the origins of the pub. It was built in 1840 by the retired head gardener of nearby Avington Park who is said to have built it with his "golden handshake". It is a bustling well-kept village local surrounded by rolling Hampshire downland where you are sure of a friendly welcome. The two little rooms have an atmosphere all of their own. Hops adorn the walls, the tables are of scrubbed pine and pews form much of the seating. For the last six years, all of the ales sold here have been brewed in the micro-brewery across the car park and very good they are too. We walked the route on a Thursday and the brewery was belching out that delicious smell of the hot wort. The traditional games of cribbage, shove halfpenny and dominoes are played in the public bar. At one time, the Flower Pots was not the only pub in Cheriton. The former HH Inn - passed on the walk, is now a private house but was once a place where "rings" was played. The game enjoyed a revival in 1959 but ceased when the pub closed some time back.

Geese at Cheriton

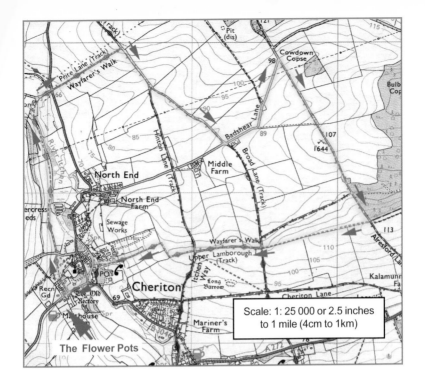

The Walk ....

Turn right from the pub and after only 100 yards (91 metres), turn left down a narrow footpath, and walk between a buttressed brick and flint wall and a cupressus hedge. Pass through the kissing gate and you will be faced with a choice of three possible ways. Take the middle of the three possible routes towards the greenish shed in the distance, which diverges slightly from the corner of the graveyard. Climb this stile, cross the little lane, climb the stile on the other side and you will notice you are on the Wayfarers Walk. This is a wide path between sheep fence and hedging. Climb a further stile and walk along the right hand side of the field following the hedge line.

You will soon hear the waters of the infant River Itchen, cross another pair of stiles, and pass under the power lines, walking parallel to the river. Climb a further stile and the footpath then becomes enclosed on either side. Walk the grassy path that looks down upon the river, pass Cheriton Mill and then turn right onto the lane and pass over the white-railing bridges. At the T-junction with the B3046, take the byway opposite which also forms the Wayfarers Walk. At the end of the byway turn right onto a further byway, and continue onward - ignoring the possible right fork at around 440 yards (400 metres), until you come to the end of the byway where you turn left onto the lane (Badshear Lane).

Just after you pass under the power lines, where Badshear Lane swings to the left, turn sharp right down another track (marked as Right of Way). After you achieve the high point of this route (by one of the mobile phone transmitters), turn right on the public footpath through the rather dilapidated wicket gate and walk along the edge of this large open field. Emerge from the field by a further wicket gate, cross straight over the track and

Resting by the Itchen

stile to the left, and take the field path along the edge of the paddock. In time, the footpath becomes sunken between hedges, and then becomes enclosed by wooden fencing. Climb over the small wooden barrier and join a short lane by Freemans Yard. Cross the river by the restricted-weight bridge, and then turn left to pass the post office. At the end of the road turn left and then immediately right to take the road signed "Bishops Waltham 7". Walk this road and you will soon find yourself back at the Flower Pots.

Weak Bridges at Cheriton

continue on a track for 500 yards (457 metres). Cross a further track and climb the stile to take the footpath on the left side of the field.

Walk along the left-hand edge of the field, you will swing right as you follow the perimeter field. About 140 yards (128 metres) after this, take the

Pub File..........

The Flower Pots: Walkers are welcome and you can get your book 'pubberstamped' here. Opening times for The Flower Pots are midday to 2.30pm and 6pm to 11pm on Mondays to Saturdays; midday to 3pm and 7pm to 10.30pm on Sundays. There is a daily 'Specials' board and a limited range of bar food available. Food times are midday to 2pm and 7pm to 9pm from Mondays to Saturdays; midday to 2pm on Sundays. Wednesday night is curry night. The pub has its own brewery 'The Cheriton Brew House'. Although children are not allowed in the pub they are welcome in the garden. Dogs are permitted if kept on a lead. Some overnight accommodation is available. Walkers are requested not to park their cars in the pub car park during winter months, however, in the summer, if the weather is fine, they may use the 3 acre (1.2 hectare) field adjoining the premises. (Tel: 01962 771318).

AN IRON AGE HILL FORT

(Where we may get wet feet and find that Winchester is not where we thought it was)

Fact File..........

Starting Point: This walk starts from the Shoe Inn at Exton.
Alternative Parking and Start Point: An alternative place to park your car is at the point where you turn off the A32 for Exton, if approaching from the north - marked as P(Alt) on the map.
Distance: Allow 2 hours 20 minutes for this walk, the distance is 4.8 miles (7.7 miles).
Classification: 'Moderate' – The walk basically consists of a climb to the top of Old Winchester Hill from river level.
Safety and Comfort: You will need to cross the A32 twice. This is a fast road so take great care when crossing. Also, the initial leg of the walk follows the course of a stream that issues from Old Winchester Hill during the winter. It is necessary to walk with your feet in the water occasionally, so waterproof footwear is essential at these times.
Maps: Ordnance Survey Landranger 1: 50 000 Series - Sheet 185.
Ordnance Survey Explorer 1: 25 000 Series - Sheet 119.
Ordnance Survey Pathfinder 1: 25 000 Series - Sheet 1265 (SU 62/72).
Map reference of start and finish - SU 612209.
Other Refreshment Possibilities: There are no other pubs on the walk. If you walk this route in the summer, there is a fair chance of buying an ice cream by the roadside at Old Winchester Hill.
Travel by Car: Exton lies just off the A32, south of Warnford.
Public Transport: The area is served hourly in the summer, and two-hourly in the winter by Solent Blue Line Bus Service No. 52 from Petersfield and Southampton (Tel: 023 80618233 or 023 80226235 for more information). There are no services on Sundays. Ray Dunn Coach Travel also operates an irregular Service No. 132 (Tel: 01489 797990 for more information).

Background ....

This walk is basically an ascent and descent of Old Winchester Hill and offers views that are as good as any others you will find in this series of walks and rides. The outgoing route that forms the early part of the ascent of Old Winchester Hill, shares its course with a spring fed stream that discharges into the River Meon and the nature of the walk therefore varies according to the time of year. In wet winters, when the springs rise, the long footpath follows the side of a watercourse. In the summer, the nature of the walk changes and the watercourse is completely dry. The directions that follow were originally written in a wet winter, so you will just have to use your imagination on a hot summer's day.

The reason that this hill is called Old Winchester Hill is difficult to explain, as it is not really close enough to the old city to have taken its name from it. There are many

Views for miles from Old Winchester Hill

An Old Winchester Hill information board

theories, and perhaps the simplest one is that its current name has come from a corruption of an earlier name - Windover Hill. The hill fort was built in the last 500 years BC (Iron Age), and encloses 5.7 hectares (14 acres) within the rampart walls. Before the building of the fort, there was already a Bronze Age burial site here. The site has not been formally excavated, but most of the barrows have been dug into.

Give-me-Five Treasure Hunt

This must be done from the top of Old Winchester Hill. There are good views from here on a fine day and so we would like you to obtain the distances in miles to these places that you should be just able to see (you will find the answers easy once you get there!):

1. Beacon Hill (the closer one).

2. Privett Church.

3. Southampton.

4. Calshot Power Station.

5. Beacon Hill at Highclere.

The associated nature reserve contains a good mixture of chalk habitat, including open grassland and woodland, containing juniper, yew, and beech. In addition to the views, the reserve has a wide selection of wild flowers, trees and shrubs, but conservation is the theme here so please do not pick flowers, or leave litter.

One final pleasure at the end of this walk is the opportunity to sit in the garden of the Shoe afterwards, look back at Old Winchester Hill in the distance, and admire your achievement. The garden is set away from the pub and at its foot is the clear and fast-flowing River Meon with a few ever-present ducks to entertain the children. It is, without doubt, a lovely place to be on a warm summer's day.

The Walk ....

From the Shoe, turn left and walk through the village, roughly parallel

with the River Meon. After about 700 yards (640 metres), you will meet the A32. Cross this taking great care, as this is a fast road, and walk along the track marked "No Through Road", and cross over the footbridge. Continue walking and just before Shavards Farm turn left where it states "Footpath Only No Horses". The path continues on for approximately 400 yards (366 metres), and eventually you arrive at the disused railway line. Climb over the embankment by using the steps at the left side of the bridge. This is the Old Meon Valley Railway Line that we visit elsewhere in this book on one of our cycle rides. It has been converted for use by walkers and cyclists and is most useful as it facilitates many additional possibilities for circular walks and rides. Proceed

down the embankment on the other side and climb over the stile. Continue along on the left hand side of the stream. You will have to cross the stream to the other bank. At one time there were stepping-stones here, but in recent months they seem to have disappeared. After a short distance you cross back again.

At a small junction, you emerge from the wooded path onto a wider track - look for the small yellow plastic arrows on the low wooden post. At the time of walking the track was awash with water and in fact formed part of the stream. You then come to a T Junction and turn right as directed by yellow arrows. The route proceeds up the hill, initially on a concrete farm track and then on a tree-covered pathway. When you emerge, the track takes a left for 100 yards (91 metres) or so and then right again. Proceed until you are forced to take a sharp left turn, and walk between a fence on the left and thicket on the right toward the yew trees marking the nature reserve.

Pass through the small swing gate that forms the entrance to the reserve, and carry straight on through the yew wood. Climb over the stile by the gate and you are in the open and almost at the top. Carry straight on to the triangulation point. Although only 646 feet (197 metres) high, the view from here is one of the best you will find in Hampshire.

Having enjoyed the views, walk on past the pond on the left, and pass through the gap in the hill fort enclosure, then turn immediately right and follow the perimeter fence of the nature reserve until you meet a stile. Climb over the stile or pass through the gate and take an angular route following the line of the very short posts down the hill, until you meet the next stile at the bottom. Climb over the stile to turn immediately right (there was no footpath indicator at the time of walking). Follow the line of the hedgerow for about 200 yards (183 metres) on its left and then for the next 300 yards (274 metres) on its right. Your route then turns sharp left and you should continue toward the row of pine trees, until you meet a footpath sign where you turn right and follow the trackway to Harvestgate Farm. At the farm, turn right onto the metalled lane, ignore the lane off to the left, and carry straight on. The lane now narrows, and then turns sharply to the right, you then go through a gap in the embankment that was once an old railway bridge. Bear left at the junction and proceed up the hill, then carry straight on until you come to the A32 again.

Cross the A32, taking great care, and go down Beacon Hill Lane back to Exton, bear right and you are back at the Shoe Inn.

Entrance to the reserve

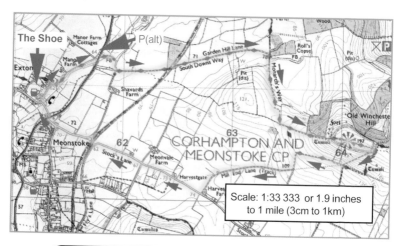

Scale: 1:33 333 or 1.9 inches to 1 mile (3cm to 1km)

Pub File..........

The Shoe at Exton: Walkers are welcome and you can get your book 'pubberstamped' here. Opening times are 11am to 3pm and 6pm to 11pm Mondays to Saturdays; midday to 3pm and 7pm to 10.30pm on Sundays. An extensive range of bar food is available and a daily 'Specials' board. Food is available from midday to 2pm and 7pm to approx. 9pm Mondays to Saturdays; and from midday to 2pm on Sundays. The pub serves real ale. Children are welcome and are allowed into at least one area of the premises. Dogs are permitted if kept on a lead. The licensee is happy for walkers to park their cars in the car park providing they patronise the pub before or after their walk. (Tel: 01489 877526).

THE HEAD OF THE MEON VALLEY

(Where we enjoy the views from Tegdown Hill and find the source of the River Meon)

Fact File..........

Starting Point: This walk starts from Ye Olde George Inn at East Meon.

Alternative Parking and Start Point: There are no public car parks around the route. If you do not wish to park in the pub car park, then there is a public car park on the west side of the village – see map. It is also possible to park in the village, but please park carefully to avoid causing any obstruction.

Distance: Allow 3 hours, the distance is 6 miles (9.7 km).

Classification: 'Moderate' – There is only one significant but gentle climb on this walk.

Safety and Comfort: No problems.

Maps: Ordnance Survey Landranger 1: 50 000 Series - Sheets 185 and 197.
Ordnance Survey Explorer 1: 25 000 Series - Sheet 119 and 120.
Ordnance Survey Pathfinder 1: 25 000 Series - Sheet 1285 (SU 61/71) & 1265 (SU 62/72).
Map reference of start and finish - SU 680222.

Other Refreshment Possibilities: In addition to Ye Olde George Inn there is the Izaak Walton, also in East Meon.

Travel by Car: Turn off the A3M to Clanfield and take the road out of Clanfield that is signposted to East Meon.

Public Transport: The village is served hourly by Stagecoach Hampshire Bus Service No. 67 from Winchester and Petersfield (Tel: 01256 464501 for more information). It is also served hourly (in the summer) by Solent Blue Line Service No. 52 from Southampton and Petersfield – services are less frequent in the winter (Tel: 023 80618233 or 023 80226235 for more information).

Background ....

We have always been particularly fond of East Meon as it is one of the finest and most attractive downland villages

East Meon Church

in Hampshire, and we make no excuse for starting two walks in this series from the same village. If you stand on Park Hill, which is to the north of the village just behind the church, it almost seems possible to reach out and touch the spire, and it is this proximity to the village of the smooth green rolling downs that makes East Meon such an attractive place. The highest hill is of course Butser Hill, but there are others that do not fall far short - nearby Salt Hill and Hyden Hill.

The Meon Valley is so-named after the Jutish tribes who founded the kingdom of the Meonwaras in this fertile valley. They are thought to have settled here in Roman Britain and to have come from the lowlands of North Germany. The natural geographical barrier of the ancient Forest of Bere, which was part of the great Anderida Forest meant that the Meonwaras' settlements flourished and remained independent throughout many of the successive invasions that swept the land after the Romans withdrew.

The highest point of this walk is Tegdown Hill which is a chalk down that overlooks East Meon and the head of the Meon Valley below. It is 722 feet (220 metres) high and along it runs the Winchester to Buriton section of the South Downs Way. One of the beauties of this walk is that the climb to the top of one of the highest hills of Hampshire is very gentle, and only gets slightly steeper at the end.

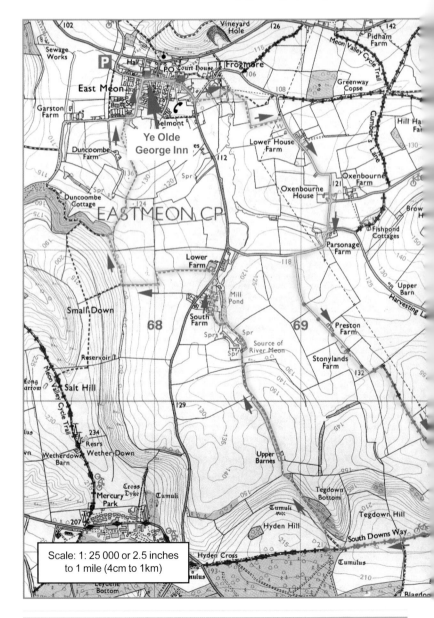

Scale: 1: 25 000 or 2.5 inches to 1 mile (4cm to 1km)

On this walk we also pass the spring holes where the River Meon rises and begins its gentle flow through the villages of the Meon Valley eventually arriving at Titchfield. Although in recent years the sinking of boreholes in the area has reduced the flow of the upper reaches significantly, there is no water as clear as that which rises from a chalk spring and none so cool for refreshing your feet after a hot summer walk in the downs.

The Walk ....

Standing with Ye Olde George Inn behind you, face right and then turn  immediately left to follow the line of the River Meon and take the road to Clanfield. Soon after you pass the post office you will see the East Meon Forge. Turn left here and then take the footpath immediately right into the recreation ground to follow the footpath that runs across the cricket ground.

Leave the cricket ground by climbing the stile, and climb a further stile to walk a narrow grassy path to cross the infant River Meon. Climb the stile ahead of you, and immedi-  ately turn right to walk initially parallel with the fence. Pass through a row of trees that look as if they once formed a boundary and then take the right-most of the two stiles. You should now follow the row of trees towards the pylon in the distance.

Climb a further stile to follow the left bound-ary of the next field and on the left you will see (re-assuringly) a fingerpost indicating that you should swing around left to continue to follow the left hand boundary of this field. Climb the stile and pass under the power lines. Climb a further stile and descend the steps to a lovely sunken lane and turn right.

At the junction (with triangular grassy island) continue as directed to "East Meon 1½" and at the next junction turn right as directed to East Meon and Clanfield. A hundred yards or so after passing under power lines turn left along a surfaced lane marked by a partially hidden sign "no through road for motor vehicles". This is a charming lane where you will eventually spy a pebble-dashed farm house and some brick farm buildings. At this point the lane becomes an unsurfaced track - continue until you are faced with two gates when you should swing left and fairly soon right to climb up onto Tegdown Hill. After about ½ mile (0.8km) the route becomes more enclosed with small trees.

At the top of the hill you will meet a block-walled and corrugated asbestos-roofed barn, turn right here to join the South Downs Way and enjoy the fine views of the head of the Meon Valley below. After ½ mile (0.8km) you will see a fingerpost and a stile that leads you away to the right at a slight angle from the South Downs Way. You will soon see the start of a slightly sunken track which you should follow until you pass through a green gate at the foot of the hill, and then pass through a further gate to continue along the pleasant track accompanied by a beautiful avenue of beech trees.

You will come upon a pair of cottages called Springholes. In the deep combe below there are springs which mark the rising of the River Meon. Continue along the concrete

Keep alert as you walk around the route and you will find the answers to these questions in the order that they are listed below:

1. *If you add all of the mileages stated on this signpost and the answer comes to "23¾", where are you? (Give the name of the nearest building).*
2. *Where might you want to stay if you wished to give up being a vegetarian?*
3. *If you add all of the mileages stated on this signpost and the answer come to "9½", where are you? (Give the name of the nearest building).*
4. *If you add all of the mileages on this signpost and they come to "12", where are you? (Give the name of the nearest building).*
5. *Where can you find a farm name made of bent horseshoes?*

drive to pass through the farmyard of South Farm with the large barns on the left and farm house on the right. Leave the farm just before its end to take the footpath via the five-bar wooden gate which passes through a small field, and then climb the stile to turn right to proceed for a few steps along the road.

Almost immediately cross the road to turn left through the two odd-looking swing gates into Lower Farm, and left again to turn back along the road for 15 yards (14 metres), pass through the old metal bar gate and then turn right by the fingerpost. Walk up the right hand side of this field and follow the perimeter around left until you spy a gap in the hedge which enables you to continue onward along the right side of the next field. Ahead, you will see a line of trees that mark the footpath that will return you to East Meon. Pass through the six-bar galvanised metal gate to follow the direction of the line of trees (they will be on your right). You will come across a six-bar galvanised metal gate in the corner of this field, turn right through this, and then left over the stout two-stepped stile to walk along the right side of this next field.

At the end of this field the path takes you across the middle of the next field toward its highest point. Then with East Meon in your sights you meet a boundary, swing half left to follow the right side of this field - there will be a brick and flint farm house on your left. At this point you will see three distinctive red-roofed "Cornish" type houses ahead, walk toward these. Climb the stile into the informal car park for local residents by Princes Cottages. Turn right to follow the road back into East Meon.

Pub File..........

Ye Olde George Inn: Walkers are welcome and you can get your book 'pubberstamped' here. Opening times are 11am to 3pm and 6pm to 11pm on Mondays to Saturdays; midday to 3pm and 7pm to 10.30pm on Sundays. There is a restaurant and extensive range of bar food. Food is available from midday to 2pm and 7pm to 9pm on Mondays to Thursdays; midday to 2.30pm and 7pm to 9.30pm on Fridays and Saturdays; and midday to 2.30pm on Sundays. The pub serves real ale. Children are welcome and are allowed into at least one area of the premises. Dogs are permitted if kept on a lead. Some overnight accommodation is available. The licensee is happy for walkers to park their cars in the car park providing they patronise the pub before or after their walk. (Tel: 01730 823481).

AN ASCENT OF SALT HILL FROM EAST MEON

(Where we do a bit of simple map reading from a high viewpoint)

Fact File..........

Starting Point: This walk starts from the Izaak Walton pub in East Meon.

Alternative Parking and Start Point: There are no public car parks around the route. If you do not wish to park in the pub car park, then there is a public car park on the west side of the village - see map. It is also possible to park in the village, but please park carefully to avoid causing any obstruction.

Distance: Allow 2 hours for this walk, the distance is 4 miles (6.4km).

Classification: 'Moderate' - this is a fairly easy walk with just a single stiff climb of Salt Hill.

Safety and Comfort: No problems.

Maps: Ordnance Survey Landranger 1: 50 000 Series - Sheet 185.
Ordnance Survey Explorer 1: 25 000 Series - Sheet 119.
Ordnance Survey Pathfinder 1: 25 000 Series - Sheet 1265 (SU 62/72).
Map reference of start and finish - SU 682222.

Other Refreshment Possibilities: In addition to the Izaak Walton, there is Ye Olde George Inn which is also situated in the village.

Travel by Car: Turn off the A3M to Clanfield and take the road out of Clanfield that is signposted to East Meon.

Public Transport: The village is served hourly by Stagecoach Hampshire Bus Service No. 67 from Winchester and Petersfield (Tel: 01256 464501 for more information). It is also served hourly (in the summer) by Solent Blue Line Service No. 52 from Southampton and Petersfield - services are less frequent in the winter (Tel: 023 80618233 or 023 80226235 for more information).

Background ....

On this walk we climb to the top of Salt Hill, which at 755 feet (230 metres) high provides excellent views both to the east and west. The scenery in these parts is truly beautiful with the village of East Meon (our starting point for this walk) sitting in a valley surrounded on all sides by rounded chalk hills. William Cobbett, the great 19th century political campaigner and writer of Rural Rides, rode through the village in 1822 and was enchanted by its setting. He approached the village from Coombe and travelled down through Coombe Cross and described his experience thus: "We came down a long steep hill that led us winding round into the village, which lies in a valley that runs in a direction nearly east and west...... If I had not seen anything further today, I should have dwelt long on the beauties of this place. Here is a fine valley, in nearly an elliptical form, sheltered by high hills sloping gradually from it ......" .

As far as the naming of the pub is concerned, we are not sure whether Izaak Walton fished in the immediate locality. We have read that he did, although he only came to live in nearby Winchester in his last years, and is buried in the south transept of the cathedral. The pub has only been named the Izaak Walton in comparatively recent years, its previous incarnation being the New Inn.

The layout of East Meon is interesting as it is fairly regular and appears to have been formally laid out, (possibly as early as the twelfth century) on the land south of the church, including a space for a small market area. One of the oldest buildings in the village is the medieval Court House. It was restored earlier this century and is used occasionally by local players for theatrical performances. Probably the oldest building in the village is the Norman church, with its noble spire that can be seen for many miles. Inside there is a stone marked "Amens Plenty" which is believed to cover the grave of Parliamentary soldiers killed during a small civil war skirmish before the Battle of Cheriton. The church also attracts William Cobbett's attention in Rural Rides and causes him to enter one of his frequent literary harangues, using the size of East Meon church to argue that at one time the village population was much larger. "Where did the hands come from to make it?" he asks. He was firmly of the belief that the country's population was decreasing, despite parliamentary returns to the contrary. In typical outspoken fashion, he wrote that anyone who believed that the population had increased in the last 20 years would "believe that the moon is made of green cheese".

Give-me-Five Treasure Hunt

*Shown below are images of 4 farms and 1 feature taken with a zoom lens from the Stone Seat at Point **X** on the map. All of the places can be found on the map, so all you need to do is link the images with what you can see in the valley below. Then roughly orientate the map so that you can locate the farm or feature on the map and therefore identify its name.*

1. ---------- ----

2. ----- ----

3. ----- ----

4. ----- ----- ----

5. ---------- ----

The Walk ....

Follow the road marked to Coombe and Chidden Down. You will pass the village school and then the road will turn sharp right. Take the first footpath off to the left that initially passes through a small enclosure that is used as a car park by villagers. Climb the stile into the field and undertake the steady climb up the hill. You will come to a further stile (broken at the time of walking) and here you will continue along the left edge of the field. After about 250 yards (229 metres), you will need to turn half right (as directed by the fingerpost). At the next fingerpost continue straight on, again following the field boundary on the left edge of the field.

You will arrive at a stout stile in the corner of the field. Turn right here, pass through the six-bar metal gate and follow the left (eastern) edge of the field for 350 yards (320 metres) or so, with Salt Hill rising steeply to your right and a narrow strip of woodland to your left. At the next six-bar gate there is a choice of routes, turn right and walk up the hill with

The shady track on a hot summer's day

the fence and the occasional stunted hawthorn tree on your left. (You will see a stone seat with excellent views to the east - you will need to sit here to answer the Give-me-5 Treasure Hunt). You will climb one stile during the ascent of the hill and you should then continue on with sheep fencing on your left. On the very summit of Salt Hill you will see a three-way fingerpost sign. Turn left here through the six bar metal gate and walk along the ridge of the hill.

At the next (similar) gate, there is a fingerpost directing you right. Proceed this way, skirting the edge of the stunted hawthorn copse to cross another track at the head of a combe. Having crossed the combe, you will meet a solidly-constructed stile that you should climb to gain access to a lovely old byway - turn right here.

At first this byway is open in aspect, and you then walk along the length of a pleasant narrow strip of

East Meon Church

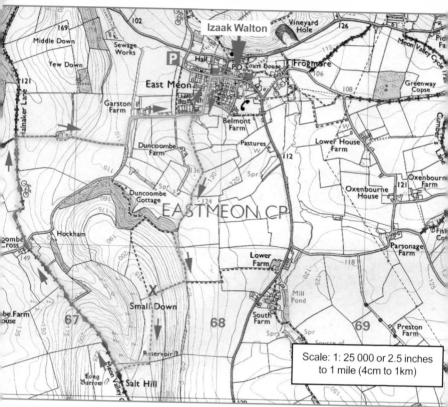

woodland. You will meet a lane at Coombe Cross, which you should cross and carry on in a similar direction (this is part of the South Downs Way). About ½ mile after crossing the lane, you will see a fingerpost sign on the right. Turn off the byway here towards the farm buildings on the sky line. The path takes you around the right side of Garston Dairy to join the farm drive that takes you to the road. At the road, turn left and re-trace your steps into East Meon.

Pub File..........

The Izaak Walton: Walkers are welcome and you can get your book 'pubberstamped' here. Opening times are 11am to 2.30pm and 6pm to 11pm on Mondays to Saturdays; midday to 10.30pm on Sundays. There is a restaurant, an extensive range of bar food and a daily 'Specials' board. Food is available from midday to 2pm and 7pm to 9pm on Mondays to Saturdays; midday to 2pm and 6pm to 8pm on Sundays. The pub serves real ale. Children are welcome and are allowed into at least one area of the premises. Dogs are permitted if kept on a lead. The licensee is happy for walkers to park their cars in the car park providing they patronise the pub before or after their walk. (Tel: 01730 823252).

A PLEASANT RAMBLE VIA ROWLANDS CASTLE
(And where we learn a little about some old Hampshire customs)

Fact File..........

Starting Point: This walk starts from the George Inn at Finchdean.

Alternative Parking and Start Point: Another suitable point for starting this walk is Rowlands Castle. Park by the roadside around the village green area - only the area closest to the shops has a time limit.

Distance: Allow 2 hours 15 minutes for this walk, the distance is 5.5 miles (8.8 km).

Classification: 'Moderate'.

Safety and Comfort: No problems.

Maps: Ordnance Survey Landranger 1: 50 000 Series - Sheet 197.
Ordnance Survey Explorer 1: 25 000 Series - Sheet 120.
Ordnance Survey Pathfinder 1: 25 000 Series - Sheet 1285 (SU 61/71).
Map reference of start and finish - SU 738127.

Other Refreshment Possibilities: Opportunities for refreshments on this walk are plentiful. In addition to the George Inn at Finchdean, there is the Coffee Pot and also three pubs in Rowlands Castle.

Travel by Car: Assuming travel from Portsmouth or the north, via the A3M, take the Horndean/Emsworth exit. Cross over the motorway following the directions to Horndean and Emsworth. Take the next left (B2149) toward Horndean and next right (signposted Finchdean). From this point just follow the directions to Finchdean.

Public Transport: Finchdean is not served by buses or trains, but the walk could be started from Rowlands Castle (please refer to Walk 9 for Rowlands Castle public transport information).

Background ....

If you were to draw a straight line on a map from Petersfield to Havant, it would pass through Finchdean. This lovely village is surrounded on all sides by gentle chalk hills. The largest of these is Idsworth Down to the north (we tackle this in another chapter), with Wick Hanger to the west and a gentler slope to the east, apparently not of sufficient importance to warrant a name.

Although it is an attractive settlement, it is not what one would call a picture postcard village; there are no large or grand houses, few thatched dwellings that we can recollect and there is, quite rightly, just a little industry - not the huge steel framed and aluminium clad boxes that proliferate these days, but buildings of a more human scale.

At the centre of things, sitting in a perfect position to keep a watchful eye on the village green and everything that passes through the village is the George

*Finchdean Hocktide Festival
1988*

Inn. We are not sure of the age of the current building, but the proceedings of the Finchdean Hundred records the sale of "all that cottage or dwellinghouse, brewhouse, stable, garden, orchard and all the other outhouses, with about one acre of ground, part of the mast of the said manor of Idsworth", in 1783 with an indication that it originally existed as far back as 1740. This sale was to a William Marshall who also owned some land in the vicinity of the green known as Marshall's Piece. It would appear that Marshall, who was probably a blacksmith, bought the inn for the accommodation of riders of horses waiting for shoeing and as a resting-place for weary travellers.

Perhaps one of the most interesting aspects of Finchdean is the Hocktide Festival that is still, we believe, held here early in May. This was staged in the Finchdean Hundred up until 1651 and revived in the late 1980s. Although for practical purposes it is now held on the May Day Bank Holiday, it was

originally held on the second Monday and Tuesday after Easter. It is a festival that marks the coming of spring, and in the old days the village was decorated, bounds were walked to establish land ownership and various forest rights, and hocked animals were released from their winter quarters to enjoy the freedom of the new grass, which probably gave the festival its name.

On Hock Monday, the women seized and bound men found on the public roads with ropes, demanding a token payment for their release; on Hock Tuesday the roles were reversed and it was the men's turn. Another charming feature was that the local men met to give Frankpledge - also known as Frithborth - where they promised good behaviour and helpful ways and gave a public account of their behaviour.

The event has changed over the years and the emphasis is now on village crafts and pastimes. So if you visit the village at Hocktide on a May Day Bank Holiday, you will not risk being kidnapped or having to give a public account of yourself.

The George Inn - Finchdean

Give-me-Five Treasure Hunt

This quiz is about dates. All you need to do is be observant and you will be able to answer all of these questions (they are not in order):

1. *What was founded in 1902?*
2. *What was built in 1914?*
3. *What was built in 1782?*
4. *When were the residents of Rowlands Castle "Good Neighbours"?*
5. *When was Mr Gibbs born?*

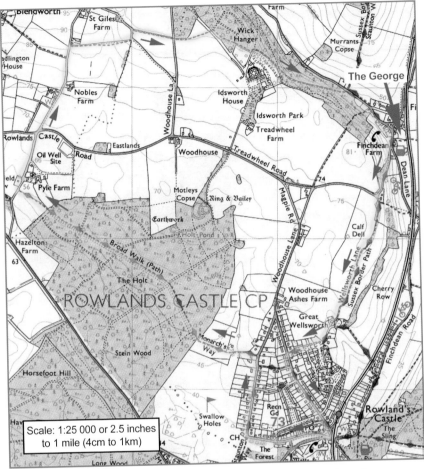

The Walk ....

From the George Inn Car Park, turn left to face a steep climb up White Hill (unmarked). At the top of the hill, where the road turns sharply right, take the footpath off to the left that is also part of the Staunton Way. After about 30 yards (33 metres), you will pass around the right hand side of a wide metal gate and then the remains of a further gate.

At this point you will join a grassy route that separates two fields. Leave the fields by passing around a further gate and turn right at the three way junction (the finger may be missing from the fingerpost), to continue along the route of the Staunton Way along Wellsworth Lane with its attractive houses. At the end of the lane turn left and follow the road (Bowes Hill) to the village green. Turn right at the bottom of the hill and you will find yourself at the village green.

Locate Links Lane at the end of the green. Follow this lane (passing the village hall and golf club house) for about 0.5 mile (0.8 km). Immediately after Holt Gardens, turn left, climb the stile (if the gate is shut) and walk the gravel track toward the golf course. Bear left onto the golf course, as indicated by the footpath fingerpost. Walk at first with the conifers on your right, before crossing a fairway (play is left to right), and then walk with a row

Rowlands Castle

on the right and take the public footpath (by the flint cottage), and walk with the field boundary on your left toward the dung heap in the distance.

At the end of the field, take the stout stile (if the gate is closed) and turn left onto the narrow lane for about 50 yards (55metres), then turn right to take the footpath on the left of this field. Cross a further narrow lane to climb a further stile and walk with the wood on your left. Climb the stile marking the end of the field - now you must be careful here to make sure that you do not lose your way. After the stile take about 23 paces and then turn right as indicated by the fingerpost.

Follow the track through the wood, which may be muddy. After crossing a track, you will eventually be joined by a 'pig-wire' fence on your right. At the end of the fence, bear left and follow the track, which after 20 yards (22metres) bends to the right and then proceeds down through Wick Hanger to the road. Leave the wood by passing through the gap by the gate to walk back into Finchdean.

of hawthorn trees on your right before crossing a further fairway (play is right to left). Please take care to co-operate with golfers as you cross the course and thereby achieve harmonious relationships. You now enter the wood known as The Holt.

Follow the well-defined footpath known as Broad Walk for about 1 mile (1.6km) in a roughly north-westerly direction, crossing a couple of tracks as you go. At the end of the wood, climb the stout stile and cross the field, walking with the two trees on your right. Climb the stile on the left of the green six-bar metal gate to turn right onto the road. Follow this road until you come to a cross-roads - and carefully cross straight over to take the road signposted to Blendworth. After about 0.5 mile (0.8km), climb the stile

Pub File..........

The George Inn: Walkers are welcome and you can get your book 'pubberstamped' here. Opening times are 11am to 3pm and 6pm to 11pm. Food is available from an extensive menu, and the specials board is changed every 2-3 days. Food is available every day from midday to 2pm and 7pm to 10pm. Children are welcome but must be seated in the front bar of the pub. There is no outside play area available. Dogs are permitted at the landlord's discretion. Some overnight accommodation is available. The licensee is happy for walkers to park their cars in the car park, providing they patronise the pub before or after their walk, but if cars are already parked there, then please use the back field as space in the car park is limited. (Tel: 023 92412257).

A STROLL IN THE FOREST

(A short circular walk around Stansted Forest from Rowlands Castle)

Fact File..........

Starting Point: This walk starts at the Castle Inn, situated immediately by the railway bridge.

Alternative Parking and Start Point: If you are not planning to visit the Castle Inn, park by the roadside around the village green area - only the area closest to the shops has a time limit.

Distance: Allow 2 hours 30 minutes for this walk, the distance is 5.0 miles.

Classification: 'Easy' - this is a gently undulating walk with no major climbs.

Safety and Comfort: No problems.

Maps: Ordnance Survey Landranger 1: 50 000 Series - Sheet 197.
Ordnance Survey Explorer 1: 25 000 Series - Sheet 120.
Ordnance Survey Pathfinder 1: 25 000 Series - Sheet 1285 (SU 61/71).
Map reference of start and finish - SU 734107.

Other Refreshment Possibilities: In addition to the Castle, there are two other pubs in the village as well as the Coffee Pot.

Travel by Car: Rowlands Castle lies about 6 miles north of Havant on the B2149. From the A3M use Junction 2 and follow the B2149 until you see signs for the village.

Public Transport: The village is served on Mondays to Saturdays by Bus Service 27 from Havant (Contact Emsworth and District Buses on 01243 378337 for further information). Travel by train is also very convenient as the village station is on the Portsmouth to Waterloo main line and the station is only a few steps from the starting point of the walk (Tel: 0345 484950 for train times).

Background ....

We can think of few places in Hampshire that provide such an excellent base to start a country walk. Not only is the village situated close to beautiful forest and chalk downland which have some of the best walks in Hampshire, it is also served by a main line rail station, and a local bus service. Parking for cars is easy as well, with on-road parking available around the green. The choice of three pubs and an excellent coffee shop means that your needs can be well catered for.

A lot of people wonder whether there ever was a castle in "Rowlands" and if so what happened to it. The castle was a Norman motte and bailey type of which nothing now remains. Before the coming of the railways, there was still some stonework at a favourite spot known as the "Dell", a picnic place for visitors who visited the village in their carriages, and then walked in the countryside. However, the building of the railway embankment to the south of the viaduct in the 1850s completely destroyed this site. The large Victorian residence known as "Deerleap" that is situated next to Rowlands Castle Hardware covers up further remains, and this is where the castle was situated. Although not possible to visit it, behind Deerleap there is a flagpole on a grassy mound that marks the spot as an ancient monument.

The history of the village is made colourful by the story of the unfortunate brutal murder of two customs men, who were met at the Castle Inn (then named the White Hart Inn and a short distance from its present site) by the notorious Hawkhurst Gang who dragged them through the countryside by horse, and beat and whipped them. One of the men met his end in a shallow grave near Rake, while possibly still alive, and the other was thrown down a well at Lady Holt Park. As he was not dead either, the gang threw large stones and timbers down on him until they had finished him off.

Evidence of Stansted Forest can be traced back to Roman times and a hunting lodge was built here for the Earl of Arundel in the 11th Century. Stansted House is the seat of the Earl and Countess of Bessborough who donated the estate to the Stansted Park Foundation in 1983. This charitable trust manages the estate for the benefit of the public, and seems to set an excellent example of economic forestry co-existing harmoniously with an amenity that the public can enjoy without charge. As a consequence of the well-managed nature of the forest, there are always sections that are subject to re-planting or re-generation. *(Background historical information drawn from Rowlands Castle Past and Present by Mary Jane Lomer and published by Lomer Enterprises).*

The Walk ....

In this walk, small engraved arrows on wooden posts are used for waymarking. Public Bridleways are represented by blue arrows and public footpaths by yellow arrows. With your back to the Castle Inn, head left to follow the Finchdean Road.

The track along the forest edge

At the point where the road bends to the left, cross it and enter the wood and you will have a choice of three footpaths. Take the footpath that goes left and immediately crosses a ditch via a plank bridge. After 60 yards (55 metres) it crosses another larger ditch (no plank bridge). The path soon runs along the edge of a fairly dense wood. You then climb a stile at the edge of the wood and walk around the right hand side of the field to gradually gain height (passing an old pair of brick and flint cottages on the right) One hundred yards (91 metres) after passing these cottages, turn right (this is very easy to miss as it is only marked by a small green arrow at the time of walking), and then left to continue following the edge of the field.

Climb the stile by the disused pit, and after a few yards you will be in an open field again. The field and path

Coloured waymarker post

gently slope downhill and you will see a pink house ahead of you (Drews Farm). Leave the field by climbing a further stile to walk along the edge of the wood, and pass another disused pit. Immediately in front of you are footpath signs and a stile. Proceed over the stile and then straight on to skirt the edge of the wood with Drews Farmhouse away to your left. For a while the route follows a narrow strip of grassland roughly 30 yards (27 metres) wide. Climb the stile to enter the next narrow field and then walk diagonally downhill to cross the corner of the field. Here you will see another stile which you should climb to follow the public footpath through the thicket. Continue meandering through this thicket for about ¼ mile (400 metres) and keep your eyes open for the fingerpost directing you left to the stile at the edge of the wood. Leave the thicket using the stile, and continue in roughly the same direction, thereby leaving the Staunton Way Circular Walk that would otherwise take you up the hill to the road.

After about 100 yards (92 metres), with a metal bar gate on your right,

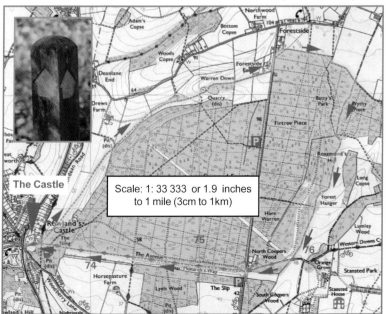

The Castle

Scale: 1: 33 333 or 1.9 inches to 1 mile (3cm to 1km)

A Stansted Park Lodge House

climb over the next stile through a tunnel of low trees and walk up an incline. By the brick and flint house, ignore the footpath off to the right, and go straight on, gradually climbing the hill.

You then join a stony track - this doubles as a drive to the brick and flint house. Keep on this track until you meet the metalled lane at Forestside.

Turn left onto this lane for about 120 yards (110 metres), then turn right into another part of Stansted Forest. Follow the footpath for a further 120 yards (110 metres) to the point where the footpath bears right and then skirts around the edge of the wood with a hedge on your left (avoid any gates or stiles that leave the wood). This path continues in a straight line for about 500 yards (457 metres). Bear right by a second swing gate, and after another 60 yards (55 metres), you come to a footpath junction. Take the left turn here, and the footpath skirts around the edge of the field with the forest on your right.

At the next crossing of routes turn right onto the bridleway. This bridleway is wide and straight for about 550 yards (503 metres), keep to this bridleway continuing to follow the blue arrows until you reach the edge of the forest, where you turn right to follow the forest edge. Continue following the edge of the forest for about 1000 yards (920 metres) until you meet a wooden gate. Turn right onto the drive that takes you away from Stansted House and brings you to the lodge house by the road to Forestside.

Cross the road, pass through the kissing gate and walk straight down The Avenue - a wide and grassy clearing in the forest. You should take the opportunity to glance back regularly for splendid views of Stansted House receding in the distance. The forest on either side has a delightful mixture of broadleaved trees - with some beautifully formed oak and beech trees. At the end of The Avenue, enter the wood and carry on in the same direction as you were going along The Avenue. Walk down the gentle slope, straight across the tarred path and you will find yourself back at the Finchdean Road, where you will be able to re-trace your steps back to the Castle Inn.

Pub File..........

The Castle Inn: Walkers are welcome and you can get your book 'pubberstamped' here. Opening times are 11.30am to 3pm and 6pm to 11pm on Mondays to Thursdays; 11.30am to 3pm and 5pm to 11pm on Fridays; 11.30am to 11pm on Saturdays; midday to 10.30pm on Sundays. There is a restaurant and an extensive range of bar food. Food is available from midday to 2pm and 7pm to 9pm on Mondays to Saturdays; midday to 2pm on Sundays. The pub serves real ale. Children are welcome and are allowed into at least one area of the premises. Dogs are permitted if kept on a lead. Some overnight accommodation is available. The licensee is happy for walkers to park their cars in the car park providing they patronise the pub before or after their walk. (Tel: 023 92412494)

ANCIENT HAMPSHIRE

(Where we discover three treasures, an ancient pub, an ancient church and an ancient track)

Fact File..........

Starting Point: This walk starts at The Red Lion, Chalton.
Alternative Parking and Start Point: There is little opportunity for alternative parking, either in Chalton or on the route. We started the walk early in the morning and were unable to use the car parks at the Red Lion as the chains were still across. We were therefore forced to park at the foot of Chalton Down, (as indicated on map). This is not a formal car park, so please take care not to obstruct the gateways, but there is room there for a car or two.
Distance: Allow 2 hours 50 minutes for this walk. The distance is 5.6 miles (9km).
Classification: 'Could make you puff' - there are a couple of steep climbs.
Safety and Comfort: If you walk the route in the winter or early spring when the lavants are up, the area around Idsworth Church and Heberdens Farm is likely to be very wet making waterproof footwear essential.
Maps: Ordnance Survey Landranger 1: 50 000 Series - Sheet 197.
Ordnance Survey Explorer 1: 25 000 Series - Sheet 120.
Ordnance Survey Pathfinder 1: 25 000 Series - Sheet 1285 (SU 61/71).
Map reference of start and finish - SU 731160.
Other Refreshment Possibilities: There are no other refreshments on the actual route.
Travel by Car: Turn off the A3M north of Horndean and follow signs to Chalton.
Public Transport: Travel by bus to Chalton is not feasible. However, Stagecoach Coastline run an hourly service between Portsmouth and Petersfield (No. 38) that serves the nearby A3.

Background ....

Like most English villages, the two most notable features in Chalton are the pub and the church. It is no accident that the two are so close together. In Chalton as in many other English villages, the pub was originally built as a workshop for the artisans employed on the rebuilding of the church. Many authorities say that the Red Lion is the oldest pub in Hampshire dating from 1147 and the site is also mentioned in Domesday. The pub's name comes from the crest of John of Gaunt who was once lord of the manor here. Being of such antiquity it is not surprising that there are many stories featuring the pub. Looking at an old copy of the church guidebook recently, we were reminded that at one time, in common with many other villages in England, the village had a benefit club. It was common to have an annual celebration and in Chalton's case this was always the second Tuesday in July. On one particular occasion, some of the villagers refused to go back and sat

St Hubert's - the little church in the field

drinking ale in the Red Lion. To counter this and to get the workers back to their haymaking, the farmer offered to pay for all the ale in the house, if the landlord would pour it all away. Fortunately, he would not do this and the men carried on with their drinking.

This walk also provides you with the opportunity of visiting St Hubert's Church. Often known as the "little church in the field", its beauty lies in its simplicity. It was originally dedicated to St Peter and St Paul in 1053, and is named after the patron saint of hunters. Within, on the north wall of the chancel are notable wall paintings that date from around 1300 and depict scenes of St Hubert and John the Baptist.

Our third treasure is the opportunity to walk along Huckswood Lane. This track provides easy and most enjoyable walking and it is one of our favourite routes in Hampshire and West Sussex. The going is very firm and well-drained, and we have never yet met anyone else walking there. The age of old roads can be estimated by the number of tree and shrub species growing in the accompanying hedgerow. A count of the species growing alongside Huckswood Lane dates it at least from the medieval period.

The Walk ....

Cross the road from the Red Lion and walk toward the church gate, through

Give-me-Five Treasure Hunt

This treasure hunt is associated with ancient tracks. As stated in the introduction, one of the ways of identifying whether a track is ancient or not is to identify the number of different species growing in the hedgerows over a particular distance. Huckswood Lane is believed to be an Ancient Track so, when you are walking along between Point A and Point B, we would like you to find 5 different leaves from shrubs or trees growing on this stretch. And then draw, sketch or trace them, marking on them which species you think they are from. We counted and recorded about 10.

the churchyard and through another gate. Then after a further 20 yards (18 metres) climb over a stile, and walk around the right hand side of the raised bank via the markers, to the stile at the top of the field.

You will find three footpaths indicated, take the left-most one.

This footpath takes you across the field. At the limit of the field climb over a stile, cross another narrow strip of field to a further stile and clamber down the hill and at the bottom you will climb another stile to join the road. Walk along the road, across the railway bridge, and at the junction go straight on down a narrow lane - this is known as Huckswood Lane. Continue along this lane until you pass a large disused quarry on the left and at this point Huckswood Lane becomes unsurfaced and is lined by some particularly splendid beech trees. Continue on for approximately 800 yards (731 metres) after the quarry until you see a crossing bridleway.

Turn right here walking across the field, passing through one hedgerow. The bridleway is almost straight and you will come to a narrow strip of woodland marking the country road from Idsworth to Littlegreen. Turn right onto this road for 50 yards, then turn left following the bridleway up the hill to Robin Wood. Continue on this route through Robin Wood, ignoring the first turning on the left (under the power lines). At the second junction continue on to the summit of the wooded hill. At the end of the wood, you should see a blue waymarker arrow instructing you to carry straight on. Do not carry straight on here, but turn sharp right (there is an arrow indicating this way on the other side of the post) to take you downhill parallel with the western edge of the wood.

The public footpath is difficult to follow at this point and the best directions are to continue for 150 yards (137 metres) until you will come to a large tree. Bear half right at this descending diagonally downhill through Robin Wood for about 200 yards (182 metres) until you meet a trackway (quite wide), which you join by climbing the three steps down the bank and turning left. Follow this trackway for a further 50 yards (45 metres) before climbing a few steps down a further bank, passing through the barrier to leave the wood and crossing the field to the stile marking the Idsworth/Littlegreen lane.

Turn left and follow the road for about 0.5 miles (731 metres) until you come to stiles on either side of the road. Take the left one and follow the footpath around the right side of the field and climb the stile to walk to the church. Continue down the grassy church path to the road and hamlet of Heberdens below.

Until recently the path took us to Heberdens Farm, but in recent years there has been a diversion. Instead of crossing the road, turn left for about 50 yards (46 metres) and then turn right to pass under the railway line. At the other side, turn left to follow the concrete path for about 100 yards (91 metres). You then turn right to climb the hill with an avenue of coppiced hazel trees on your left. Continue to the top of the down, joining the Staunton Way and Sussex Border Path and following the left edge of the field. The path then swings right to walk in a northward direction, continuing to follow the long distance paths to the summit of Idsworth and Chalton Downs. The view from here is marvellous and extends to the sea on a clear day.

Just before crossing under the power lines, climb over the stile that takes you to the other side of the fence. The footpath is not well defined so aim for the burial mound in the middle of the field. After this the footpath roughly follows the centre line of the field, and then gradually veers to the left following the line of the hedge. A little further, and you will find yourself at the top of the field again by Chalton Church. Retrace your steps back to the churchyard, climbing the stile and gate to enter and leave. Pass through the lych gate to return to the Red Lion.

Right - Deep in thought on Chalton Down

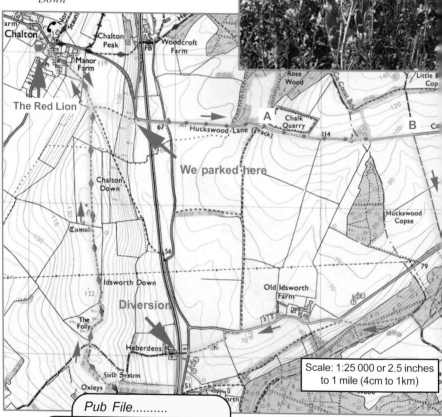

Scale: 1:25 000 or 2.5 inches to 1 mile (4cm to 1km)

Pub File.........

The Red Lion: Walkers are welcome and you can get your book 'pubberstamped' here. Opening times are 11am to 3pm and 6pm to 11pm on Mondays to Saturdays; midday to 3pm and 7pm to 10.30pm on Sundays. There is a family dining room and an extensive range of bar food. Food is available every day except on Sunday evenings. The pub serves real ale. Children are welcome and are allowed into at least one area of the premises. Dogs are permitted if kept on a lead. Walkers are requested to park their cars in the public car park next to the pub. (Tel: 023 92592246).

A WALK IN THE HILLS OVER-LOOKING PETERSFIELD

(Where we visit Little Switzerland and find that the hills have some funny names)

Fact File..........

Starting Point: This walk starts from the Harrow Inn at Steep just north of Petersfield.

Alternative Parking and Start Point: There are no public car parks around the route. However when we did our check of this route in November 2000, we were unable to drive to our planned starting point at the Harrow, due to a landslide between Steep Church and Steep Tennis Club. We parked outside Steep Church (as indicated on map) where the road is wide enough to leave your car, but please be careful not to park too close to the village school if you are walking on a school day.

Distance: Allow 2 hours, the distance is 4 miles (6.4km).

Classification: 'Moderate' - there is just one steep climb up to Wheatham Hill and Shoulder of Mutton Hill.

Safety and Comfort: No problems.

Maps: Ordnance Survey Landranger 1: 50 000 Series - Sheet 197.
Ordnance Survey Explorer 1: 25 000 Series - Sheet 133.
Ordnance Survey Pathfinder 1: 25 000 Series - Sheet Sheet 1265 (SU 62/72).
Map reference of start and finish - SU 751251.

Other Refreshment Possibilities: There are no other opportunities for refreshment on the actual walk. A short detour of about 0.7 miles into Steep village will bring you to the Cricketers Inn.

Travel by Car: Head north out of Petersfield to Steep. Turn right by The Cricketers and follow the lane for 1 mile (1.6km).

Public Transport: Travel to this walk by public transport is not easy. There is no service that takes you directly to the Harrow Inn. However, Steep village is served by Stagecoach Coastline Service No. 97 that runs on an irregular basis from Petersfield to Froxfield Green (Tel: 01903 237661 for further information).

Background ....

Steep and its surrounding combes is very much the countryside of the Edwardian writer Edward Thomas. There is scarcely a place in the area that he did not mention, either in his prose or poetry. Knowing how he liked both the Steep area and old isolated country pubs, it is surprising that The Harrow Inn does not appear in his poetry, but we are sure he must have visited from time to time. If, like us, you favour old country pubs then the Harrow is simply the best. It is a cosy convivial out-of-the-way pub, makes no concessions to the modern world and has been the same from as far back as we can remember.

This walk starts from the Harrow and heads northward onto the old chalk ridge of Wheatham and the Shoulder of Mutton Hill, an area long known by tourists as Little Switzerland. The area is characterised by a network of very old roads, lanes and paths, some of which have been severely eroded over the years by the wheels of agricultural carts. Shoulder of Mutton Hill is named we believe, after the shape of the clearing in the woods, although due to the spread of the woodland growth it does not look much like a shoulder of mutton these days. For some reason, the beech woods clinging to the hill sides around Steep, known as Hangers, have the most imaginative and charming names. Aside from Shoulder of Mutton hill, there are Happersnapper, Strawberry, Cheesecombe and Juniper Hangers.

In the clearing on Shoulder of Mutton Hill is an old sarsen stone brought from Avebury in Wiltshire and inscribed as a memorial to Edward Thomas, and placed by a path that he often walked. On the walk you will find yourself walking for some distance on the top of the hill, unable to enjoy what you know must be a superb view, as you are screened by trees. But in the end, just as you start to walk down Shoulder of Mutton Hill, and you begin to give up hope, the magnificent vista opens up before you. Edward Thomas's thought when

The lovely old Harrow Inn

he enjoyed this view were:

Yes, Sixty miles of South Downs at one glance.
Sometimes a man feels proud of them, as if
He has just created them with one mighty thought..........

The Walk ....

With your back to the pub, turn left to walk down the lane. This peters out and you then cross the Ashford Stream. You initially walk parallel with it, and then walk high up above a deeply sunken tributary of the stream. You will meet a very narrow surfaced lane on its bend where you take the left option. After 300 yards (274 metres) you will meet another lane on its bend where you turn left in a similar way to previously.

In Steep Marsh, carry straight on at the junction as directed: "Wheatham ¾, Oakshott 1½". After you leave the village, this lane becomes overshadowed by high banks on which grow lovely specimens of beech and silver birch. At the junction of lanes to Wheatham Oakshott and Steep, take the Steep lane and then at the next junction turn sharp right to take the footpath almost immediately on the left, which enables you to continue climbing Wheatham Hill. The path runs across a field and then through a pleasant little avenue of stunted trees, after which you climb a stile and turn left to join Old Litten Lane - a roughly surfaced track.

This is a very steep climb. Follow the track for about ¾ mile (1.2km) and then you will need to keep your eyes peeled to the left to look out for a red horseshoe sign. Turn left here to pass through a single bar gate and follow the red horseshoe signs. When you see the Ashford Hangers Nature Reserve sign, take the public footpath

Scale: 1:25 000 or 2.5 inches to 1 mile (4cm to 1km)

We parked here

A walk in the hills overlooking Petersfield ● **57**

Old oast houses at Steep Marsh

to the left. Climb the stile or pass around it, and the path becomes pleasantly gravelled, with the Ashford Stream trickling over a weir and through ponds on the right. Avoid any side turnings off this path (which is also the Hangers Way) until you arrive at the lane. Here turn right on the lane (water will probably be running on the left). You will come to the Mill Lane road marker, turn left here through the rather odd kissing gate and walk in the direction of the fingerpost skirting the edge of the wood on the right.

In the corner of the field, walk the planks and climb the stile to penetrate the wood. In a short distance you come upon the school playing field opposite All Saints Church. Turn left here and follow the lane that after ½ mile (0.8km) will take you back to The Harrow.

indicated by a small yellow arrow straight down through the wooden barrier until you come to the Edward Thomas memorial. Pause awhile here if you have time and enjoy the view.

Carry on straight down the steep hill and you will come to a flight of steps. Leave the nature reserve by climbing the stile. On meeting the lane at the bottom, turn right for 20 yards (18 metres) and then take the path left that follows the drive to "The Studio". The drive swings to the right - at this point take the public footpath

The Edward Thomas Memorial Stone

Pub File.........

The Harrow Inn: Walkers are welcome and you can get your book 'pubberstamped' here. Opening times are midday to 2.30pm and 6pm to 11pm on Mondays to Fridays; 11am to 3pm and 6pm to 11pm on Saturdays; and midday to 3pm and 7pm to 10.30pm on Sundays, except from October to March when the pub is closed on a Sunday evening. Food is available from a limited range of bar food every day from midday to 2pm and 7pm to 9pm, except on Sunday evenings when the pub is closed. The pub serves real ale. Although children are not permitted inside the pub they are welcome in the rear garden. Dogs are allowed in the pub if kept on a lead. The pub has such a small car park that walkers are requested to park their cars in Harrow Lane. (Tel: 01730 262685).

A WALK IN THE HILLS AROUND SELBORNE

(Where we learn a little about Gilbert White and walk in his steps)

Fact File.........

Starting Point: This walk starts from the Selborne Arms. There is a public car park immediately behind the pub.

Alternative Parking and Start Point: The Selborne Public Car Park is the only suitable car park from which to start your walk.

Distance: Allow 2 hours 45 minutes for this walk. The distance is 5.5 miles (8.8km).

Classification: 'Moderate' - The main climb is the initial one up the zig-zag steps to the top of Selborne Hill.

Safety and Comfort: No problems.

Maps: Ordnance Survey Landranger 1: 50 000 Series - 186.
Ordnance Survey Explorer 1: 25 000 Series - Sheet 133.
Ordnance Survey Pathfinder 1: 25 000 Series - Sheet 1244 (SU 63/73).
Map reference of start and finish - SU 742335.

Other Refreshment Possibilities: In Selborne there is the Queens Hotel, the Bush House Tea Rooms and also tea rooms at the Gilbert White Museum.

Travel by Car: From the A3 north east of Petersfield take the A325 to West Liss and then the B3006 to Selborne.

Public Transport: Selborne is served by Stagecoach Hampshire Bus Service No. 72 from Alton and Petersfield.

Background ....

Selborne is delightfully set beneath Selborne Hanger (or Hill) and the village is principally famous for being the birthplace and home of the 18th century naturalist Gilbert White. He lived here from 1720 to 1793 and spent most of his life in Selborne. His main interest in life was of course the observation of natural history. He was especially interested in birds and a good proportion of his writing is about the habits and behaviour of birds. He was not however restricted to this subject as he also wrote about his observations of insects, and small animals. Another of his interests was gardening and he recorded details about his gardening at The Wakes, in his 'Garden Kalendar', which was written over a twenty year period.

He is of course most famous for his 'Natural History of Selborne' a record of his correspondence with two friends on all subjects of natural history, and some not even connected with natural history. It makes fascinating reading as it gives a picture of Selborne as it was 200 years ago. It also gives the reader an insight into the level of knowledge at that time. For instance he was very concerned as to whether birds that we now know as migrants actually migrated, or whether they really hibernated during winter. Another subject that occupied his attention was the hibernation of animals and he learnt about this by studying a pet tortoise that he named Timothy.

This walk gives you the chance to experience at first hand the environment of Selborne, see where Gilbert White lived and walk up the zig-zag path that he cut himself (with the help of his brother). Also, there is plenty to see after your walk; The Wakes (this was his home and is now The Gilbert White Museum) and St Mary's Church. The church is normally open during the day and contains two stained glass windows dedicated to Gilbert White. The first illustrates St Francis of Assisi, Selborne and some of the birds mentioned in 'The Natural History of Selborne'. The second commemorates White's bicentennial anniversary. In the churchyard is the base of the famous 1400-year-old yew tree that was sadly blown down in the severe storms of 1990, and you will also find the grave of Gilbert White.

Give-me-Five Treasure Hunt

Keep alert as you walk around the route and you will find the answers to these questions in the order that they are listed below:

1. *How high does "the hill of chalk" rise above the village of Selborne?*
2. *When was the zig-zag path cut?*
3. *Who devoted his life to the service of Newton Valence?*
4. *After you cross the B3006 (Selborne Road) the bridleway is made of something unusual - what is it?*
5. *What is the meaning of "Glebe Field"?*

The Walk ....

The walk starts from the Selborne Arms. Take the footpath to the left of the car park that  takes you up to the zig-zag path and the hanger. Pass through the gate and ascend the hanger by means of the zig-zag path built by Gilbert White and his brother. At the very top of the hill (by the stone) bear right - there is a wooden bungalow on the left. You then follow the wide green path on the left through the woods for a fair distance. Eventually, you will come across a clearing on your right, which is part of Selborne Common. You will need to bear slightly left here, again following a wide green path. Unfortunately, there is no fingerpost to guide you, so you will have to be alert at this point.

As you come towards the end of the wood you will come upon a fingerpost where you carry straight on and then turn immediately right, leaving the wood and entering a field by means of a kissing gate. Walk across this field towards another stile. Climb the stile and pass into the next field, passing by the tennis court that belongs to the large house. Walk over to the far left hand corner of the field and you will see two stiles - climb the left one. Pass through the woody glade and the remains of the revolving metal gate, through the yew trees and churchyard.

About 100 yards (91 metres) after leaving the churchyard, turn right - Manor Garden House is on the right, and pass along a pleasant, mown (at the time of walking) footpath. Go through the wooden gate and walk straight across the field. At the other side of the field pass through the metal kissing gate, cross the road to pass through a similar gate and follow the footpath down the hill through very pleasant parkland. This area has some fine tree specimens and shows how man can sometimes, if he is careful, enhance the natural environment. We saw two deer at this point bounding and skipping down the hill.

Emerge from the parkland by the stile, turn right and walk along the metalled lane. Follow this lane for about 1 mile (1.6km). You need to leave the road where it turns sharply to the right. There are two possibilities - a bridleway or a public footpath. It is the latter that you need to follow and you need to walk on the right hand side of the barbed wire fence. This means that you will be on the left hand side of a field with a corrugated asbestos shed on your right. A grassy track leaves this field to the left running parallel to the field and terminates with a stile. Walk along the left of the next field, cross the stile that is situated just over half way down and diagonally cross the next small field. Cross the wide concrete

Selborne village

bridge and pass into another field, continue walking on the left hand side of this field (there will be a double row of young saplings marking the field edge). At the top of the field you will come to the road (B3006).

Cross the road, pass through the green metal bar gate and take the bridleway opposite. The bridleway eventually becomes a rutted track. At the end of the field you join a slightly sunken bridleway with a steep valley

Gilbert White Memorial Plaque

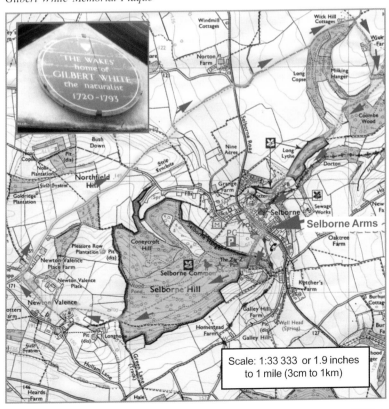

Scale: 1:33 333 or 1.9 inches to 1 mile (3cm to 1km)

Selborne Church and plaque

opening into the woods. Climb the stile to enter the woods and continue walking along the path with the barbed wire fence to your left. After about 200 yards (183 metres), you will cross a stream and come to a wooden gate and stile. Climb the stile and turn sharp left to walk downhill to the lower corner of the field. Climb this stile and cross the stream by the right-most of the two plank bridges and walk up toward the stile by the next wood.

Do not pass into the woods at this point but ignore the stile and walk left along the edge of the wood. You will soon come to another stile - enter the wood here and follow the wide gravel path along the edge of Long Lythe Wood. At the end of this wood, pass through two wooden kissing gates about 40 yards (37 metres) apart. This brings you to the Short Lythe Wood. You will be accompanied by the stream below and will pass a pretty lattice-windowed cottage. Cross the wooden footbridge across the stream to leave the Short Lythe. On leaving this wood climb the grassy hill with the oak tree and wooden seat on your right - you will soon see the church. Walk through the churchyard, admire the stump of the once great and famous yew, possibly visit the church and then carry on to the road, turn left and return to Selborne.

to the right. Leave the field by a green track and pass Wick Hill Cottages where the bridleway becomes a shingly track. At the junction with the metalled lane turn right and when you come to the farm buildings and large open barns, bear left slightly and carry on down the green lane until you come to the six bar metal gate.

Pass into the bumpy field, turn left as soon as you can and walk towards the stile at the edge of the woods. Do not climb the stile, but instead turn your back to it and walk in the direction indicated by the fingerpost toward the electricity pole in the middle of the field. Here, walk past the enclosed pond and you will see an

Pub File.........

The Selborne Ams: Walkers are welcome and you can get your book 'pubberstamped' here. Opening times vary slightly according to the season. In winter the pub is open daily from 11am to 3pm and in summer from 11am to 11pm. There is a restaurant, an extensive range of bar food and a daily 'Specials' board. Food is available every day from midday. The pub serves four different real ales. Children are welcome and are allowed into at least one area of the premises. Dogs are not permitted into the pub. (Tel: 01420 511247)

A VISIT TO KINGLEY VALE

(Where we enjoy the yews and the views)

Fact File..........

Starting Point: This walk starts from the Hare and Hounds at Stoughton.

Alternative Parking and Start Point: There are two alternatives to parking at the Hare and Hounds. It is possible to park in the village, but please park carefully. If you are willing to add a short distance to your walk, you could also park at the small public car park at West Stoke.

Distance: Allow 2 hours 30 minutes for this walk, the distance is 5 miles (8km).

Classification: 'Could make you puff' - a fairly hilly walk.

Safety and Comfort: No problems.

Maps: Ordnance Survey Landranger 1: 50 000 Series - Sheet 197.
Ordnance Survey Explorer 1: 25 000 Series - Sheet 120.
Ordnance Survey Pathfinder 1: 25 000 Series - Sheet 1286 (SU 81/91).
Map reference of start and finish - SU 804115.

Other Refreshment Possibilities: There are no other opportunities for refreshment on the walk.

Travel by Car: Stoughton is about 9 miles (14.5km) north west of Chichester and lies just off the B2147 Funtington to Petersfield road.

Public Transport: Sussex Bus No. 54A serves the village from Chichester but there are only two journeys a week. Sussex Bus Service No. 54 serves nearby Walderton every two hours. (Tel: 01903 237661 for more information).

Background ....

This walk starts from the Hare and Hounds at Stoughton. Although modernised, the pub is over 350 years old, and is a perfect starting point for a walk on the downs. Its claim to fame is that it was once run by Stirling Moss's mechanic John Brierley. It is extremely popular and we have always found it important to arrive early if you are intending to have a meal there.

The attractive village of Stoughton lies at the foot of the Kingley Vale Nature Reserve which contains one of the great Stone Age centres of the downs, and is now famous for the grove of yews which have been growing there for over a thousand years, and are probably the finest in England with girths of up to 5 metres. The yews are very gnarled and yet attractive, but because the nature of their growth largely excludes light, little grows beneath them. A good time to walk the route is in spring when the contrasting dark green of the yews and the pale green of spring leaf is very attractive. There is a small visitor centre in the reserve which explains its importance from the conservation viewpoint. The reserve contains one of the most important collections of yew trees in Europe, some of which are over 500 years old. It also has areas of chalk downland and the more unusual chalk heathland. There are 200 species of flower here, including 12 types of orchid, 57 species of breeding bird and 33 types of butterfly. There are also extensive earthworks and burial sites of Bronze Age kings from around 3000 years ago. The site is now a nature reserve controlled by English Nature.

The Walk ....

This walk is very suitable for a picnic within the nature reserve if the weather is fine. From the Hare and Hounds, turn left and walk up the lane through the village. By the property known as Old Bartons, take the public footpath to

Orchids in full bloom

Freedom on the downs

the downs. The path is a wide track and you pass various agricultural buildings on this long uphill climb. After a distance of 0.7 mile (1.1km) the climb becomes steeper, but the view as you look back toward Stoughton is worth the effort. As you approach the top of the hill the path becomes more enclosed between fencing and you will pass a seat on the left, provided by Emsworth Rambling Club. Set back from this seat, 50 yards (45 metres) or so from the path is a stone table and seats, celebrating 25 years ownership of the Stoughton Estate by the Langmead family. This

Give-me-Five Treasure Hunt

Here are five questions that can be answered around the walk. You need no prior knowledge - you just need to be observant. The questions are in the order that you come across them:

1. *Who unveiled the Langmead Memorial?*
2. *Which are the only reptiles found at the Kingley Vale reserve?*
3. *What is the kestrel's favourite food at the reserve?*
4. *What type of plane was the Polish pilot flying when he crashed and died?*
5. *When was St Mary's Church built?*

memorial is worth the short detour as it contains stones from Langmead farms from many places in the British Isles. Both of these spots are excellent sites for picnics. Very soon after these you will come to a junction of ways. Turn right here along the shingle track.

After 170 yards (155 metres) you need to be careful that you turn off left (marked as a bridleway) to take a less obvious route with conifers on the right and young beech trees on the left. The path becomes enclosed by trees on either side. Continue onward, ignoring any turnings and after about 0.5 mile (0.8km) you will come to a crossing bridleway. There is a nature reserve information board here. Cross straight over and descend the hill on a sunken and badly worn chalk track surrounded by yew trees. There are fine views ahead of the coastal plain and the sea.

We now leave the nature reserve area and take the wide fenced track down the hill for just under 0.5 mile (0.8km) where you turn right. At this

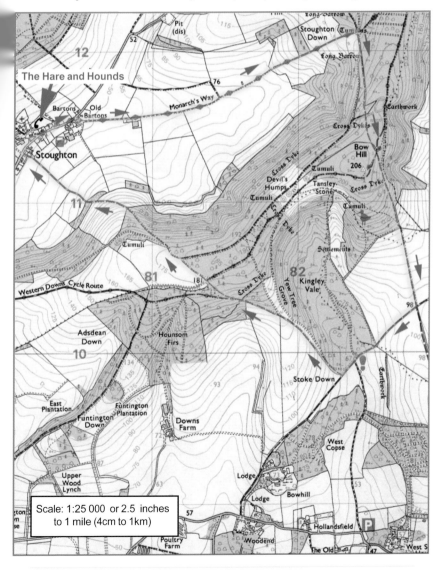

An inviting scene

point you now have the vale spread out on your right. You will soon come upon the main entry point into the reserve.

You may wish to leave the route and enter the reserve here. There is a small visitor centre which explains the importance of the reserve.

About 150 yards (137 metres) after the centre, turn right and climb up the steep hill on the well-worn track, past the "Welcome to Kingley Vale" sign. After a steep climb of 0.5 mile (0.8km) there is a fork of bridleways. Take the route that keeps to the sheep-fencing on the left. You will start to enter the wood and for a short time pass through some of the large and very old yew trees. After a further 300 or so yards (270 metres) there is a choice of two bridleways - take the right-most route indicated by the painted blue arrow. You will eventually pass through the wood to its left hand (south westerly) edge, the route becomes shingly and you commence your descent back into Stoughton.

There are some interesting stone seats on the way down and a memorial to a Polish Fighter Pilot of 213 Squadron RAF Tangmere, and of the Polish Air Force, who died aged 23 when his fighter crashed following aerial combat with a German ME109.

The bridleway eventually brings you back to Stoughton between Tythe Barn House and Jeremys. Here you turn right and walk back to the pub.

Pub File..........

The Hare and Hounds at Stoughton: Walkers are welcome and you can get your book 'pubberstamped' here. Opening times are 11am to 11pm on Fridays, Saturdays and Sundays; and 11am to 3pm and 6pm to 11pm on Mondays to Thursdays. There is a restaurant, an extensive range of bar food and a daily 'Specials' board. All meals are prepared on site and freshly cooked on the day. Food is available every day from 11am to 2.30pm and 6pm to 9.30pm. The pub serves six ales and has been in the Camra Good Beer Guide for 22 years! Children are welcome and are allowed into at least one area of the pub. Dogs are permitted if kept on a lead. The licensee is happy for walkers to park in the car park providing he is informed. (Tel: 023 92631433).

A LITTLE PIECE OF HOLLAND

(Where you will enjoy some bracing sea air and a complete lack of hills)

Fact File..........

Starting Point: This walk starts at the Old House at Home pub in Chidham.

Alternative Parking and Start Point: If you are not using the Old House at Home and its car park, the only place that we have been able to locate that is suitable for parking is Cot Lane close to the pub.

Distance: Allow 2 hours 45 minutes for this walk, the distance is 5.5 miles (8.8 km).

Classification: 'Gentle' - this is a very flat walk that would be suitable for those who are less fit.

Safety and Comfort: This walk tends to follow the embankment forming the sea defence. On the west side this is seriously crumbling away and as the embankment is elevated, it would be safer to walk on the foreshore itself to a avoid a fall. At high tides, this could mean wet feet.

Maps: Ordnance Survey Landranger 1: 50 000 Series - Sheet 197.

Ordnance Survey Explorer 1: 25 000 Series - Sheet 120.

Ordnance Survey Pathfinder 1: 25 000 Series - Sheet 1304 (SU 60/70).

Map reference of start and finish - SU 788039.

Other Refreshment Possibilities: None.

Travel by Car: Chidham is close to the A259 Havant to Chichester road. Travelling from Havant, turn right just before the Chidham sign at the Barleycorn pub, into Cot Lane. Keep following this pleasant lane to the pub.

Public Transport: Emsworth and District Bus Service No. 11 provides a 2 hourly service on weekdays from Chichester (Tel: 01243 378337) and Stagecoach Busline Service 700 serves the area from Chichester and Southsea every 30 minutes on weekdays, and hourly on Sundays (Tel: 01903 237661). Please note that the buses do not leave the A259 so you will have a short walk to get to the start.

Background ....

For this walk, we forsake the beauty of the downs to encounter a little piece of Holland wedged between Thorney Island and Bosham. To form a background to this walk, we have tried to discover a little of the history of the parish of Chidham. Every book that we have consulted has told us one thing and one thing only; Chidham is famous for its wheat, known as

Chidham White or Hedge Wheat. The reason for the latter name is tied up with the story that you are about to read. It is best told by E.V. Lucas in his Highways and Byways in Sussex: "The wheat was produced more than a century (now nearly two centuries) ago by Mr Woods, a local farmer. He noticed one afternoon (probably on a Sunday, when farmers are most noticing) an unfamiliar patch of wheat growing in a hedge. It contained thirty ears, in which were fourteen hundred corns. Mr Woods carefully saved it and sowed it. The crop was eight pounds and a half. These he sowed, and the crop was forty-eight gallons. Thus it multiplied, until the time came to distribute it to other farmers at a high price". The cultivation of Chidham Wheat at one side of the county was synchronised with the breeding of Southdown sheep by John Ellman at the other to provide two significant landmarks in agricultural history.

Pub sign showing the ears of wheat for which Chidham has a place in history

The peninsula of Chidham is a pleasant, quiet and at times windswept sort of place. There is no town or large village and if ever a place could be described as "off the beaten track", this is it. To the west of Chidham is Thorney Island. Although the RAF left Thorney in 1976, and the army have since taken their place, it still evokes the feeling that the "boys in light blue" are still there, with the airfield, control tower and hangars visible from the walk. We have the M.O.D. to thank for this unspoilt view to the west.

Finally we must turn our attention to The Old House at Home. A lovely old pub with a lovely old name. It is an appropriate name too; if one ignores the sign and obvious trappings of a pub, it has the air of a well-built, small country house. Beside being unspoilt, it can be a cosy place (after a walk around the foreshore on a cold winter's day), with rain driving against the window and flames leaping up the chimney. It is an interesting pub too, as you will find out if you can get the landlord to tell you about the smuggler's hole, and the old baker's oven in the chimney. A few years ago Old Chidham Ale was brewed here, in the brewhouse at the back, but the disappearance of this is compensated by the appearance of many good ales, that will refresh the palate of the real ale enthusiast.

The Walk ....

Chidham is only a few feet above sea level and as such it is constantly under threat from the sea. For a good part of the walk, the path follows the bank that protects the land from the sea, but in places it is crumbling, especially on the west

Give-me-Five Treasure Hunt

As you walk along the foreshore, collect five of the following, take them home and obtain an image of the items (by sketching, tracing, or taking a rubbing or photograph). It is best to start collecting after Cobnor Point.

1. *An oak leaf.*
2. *A small shell.*
3. *A larger sea shell.*
4. *A piece of seaweed.*
5. *A poplar leaf.*

side where it faces the prevailing weather. We have noticed over the last few years that the damage is worsening year by year, so it is now probably safest to walk on the foreshore from Cobnor Point onwards. Of course, during very high tides, it may be difficult to do this without getting your feet wet.

From the pub turn right to walk toward the church, and continue to follow Cot Lane until it meets Chidham Lane. Here, carry straight on initially along the gravelled path, and then go to the left side of the plant nursery. The path then becomes a field path, where you walk along the right side of the field toward Wadeway Cottage - a small and charming brick, flint and thatch building - ahead of you. Drop down the steps to the road,

turn left, walk for about 50 yards (46 metres) past the cottage and take the footpath to the right that follows the course of the road. You will walk with a tidal inlet on your left, and you should keep on to the end of the road, which looks increasingly like a private drive. By the "roundabout" you will see a public path fingerpost that takes you straight on, between high hedges, to the foreshore. Take to the footpath that runs along the sea bank. After about 0.5 mile (0.8 km) you come to a junction of paths - take the left option here that enables you to continue around the perimeter of the peninsula. You will soon come to the only, somewhat annoying, diversion that takes you away from the foreshore. This is around the Cobnor Activities Centre. The route is obvious as you

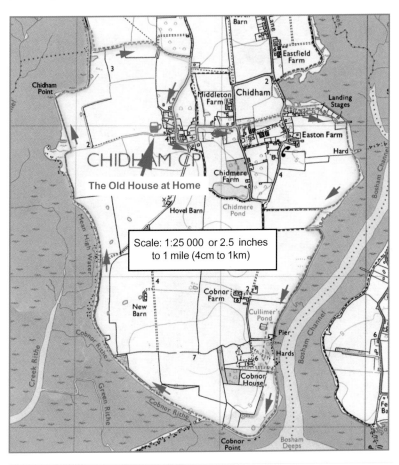

Chidham Church

---

skirt around the centre to eventually regain the line of the foreshore.

Due to the forethought of some, this next short section of the walk is surfaced to provide wheelchair access for the disabled along this pleasant section of foreshore. At Cobnor Point, you should now walk on the foreshore to pass the group of stunted and wind-shaped oak trees that grow on the margin between the foreshore and the land. The route from here follows the sea bank, but be careful as it is crumbling in places. After about 1.5 miles (2.4km) on this section you will see a footpath to the right that turns back parallel with your original route for a short distance. Take the seven steps necessary to access this route. It eventually swings inland and proceeds along the edge of an arable field with a ditch and hawthorn scrub to your right. Cross the two planks across the ditch, and carry on in a similar way in the next field and walk toward the poplar trees. You will soon meet Cot Lane, where you turn right and return to the pub.

Pub File..........

The Old House at Home: Walkers are welcome and you can get your book 'pubberstamped' here. Opening times are 11.30am to 2.30pm and 6pm to 11pm on Mondays to Fridays; midday to 3pm and 6pm to 11pm on Saturdays; midday to 4pm and 7pm to 10.30pm on Sundays. There is a restaurant, an extensive range of bar food and a daily 'Specials' board. Food is available from midday to 2pm and 6pm to 9.30pm on Mondays to Saturdays; midday to 3pm and 7pm to 9pm on Sundays. The pub serves real ale. Children are welcome and are allowed into at least one area of the premises. Dogs are permitted if kept on a lead. The licensee is happy for walkers to park their cars in the car park providing they patronise the pub before or after their walk. (Tel: 01243 572477).

THE HEART OF THE DOWNS

(Where we visit an old favourite and discover some of the best countryside in the South Downs)

Fact File..........

Starting Point: This walk starts from the Royal Oak at Hooksway.

Alternative Parking and Start Point: There is a public car park at Harting Hill and this is shown on the map.

Distance: Allow 3 hours 15 minutes for this walk, the distance is 6.4 miles (10.2 km).

Classification: 'Could make you puff'.

Safety and Comfort: No problems.

Maps: Ordnance Survey Landranger 1: 50 000 Series - Sheet 197.
Ordnance Survey Explorer 1: 25 000 Series - Sheet 120.
Ordnance Survey Pathfinder 1: 25 000 Series - Sheets 1285 and 1286 (SU 61/71 & SU 81/91).
Map reference of start and finish - SU 815162.

Other Refreshment Possibilities: This walk is set deep in the downs and there are no other pubs or tea shops nearby. However, on a summer day, although we make no promises, there is usually a good chance of an ice cream at the Harting Hill Car Park.

Travel by Car: Hooksway is situated just off the B2141, 7 miles (11.2 km) from Chichester.

Public Transport: There is no regular bus service serving the Hooksway area.

Background ....

In our view, this stretch of the South Downs is unsurpassed for its beauty. The centrepiece of the walk is a two mile (3.2 kilometre) stretch of the South Downs Way that provides some of the best views in the south of England. There is no better place to be than on the South Downs on a summer's day.

The walk starts from our favourite starting point at the Royal Oak at Hooksway. This must be the most unspoilt, beautifully-situated country pub in the land. It sits in a small, sheltered and secluded valley and being hidden away from casual passers-by, it sets a difficult challenge for the first-time visitor. A good way to start your walk on a sunny spring morning is to sit outside and enjoy a cup of coffee, listening to the bird song echoing around this wooded valley. Only the occasional rambler passes by, on his or her way to the downs.

The Royal Oak is around 400 years old but has had many additions (and subtractions). It is the place where Alfred Ainger, one of the most famous Sussex publicans, who became a legend in his own time, spent many years. Although it seems that everyone who lived within an evening's motoring trip of the pub had met him, (and can tell the famous story of the toilet which we will relate later), we found little set down on paper until we came across Bernard Price's excellent collection of articles contained in 'Sussex: People-Places-Things'. In this, he recalls meeting Alf Ainger and the information that

The South Downs

follows is largely drawn from that account.

Although his speech was of the Sussex tongue, Alf Ainger was originally a Cockney, born close to Bow churchyard. His father moved the family to Worthing in 1887 and survived the fever there in 1893. The family moved to Hooksway in 1905, he married Caroline (Carrie) in 1906 and they took over the pub in November 1907 and held it for over 50 years.

Even in the latter days of the Aingers' reign there were only oil lamps to light the small bar and a small grate, making it a cosy if rudimentary sort of place. On a Saturday night, the pub would be packed by over 80 people and the songs of Sussex could be heard ringing out across the valley.

Due to its close proximity to the West Dean estate, it was not unusual for the occasional royal visitor to drop in while on a shooting trip. King Edward VII visited The Royal Oak whilst shooting as did King Alphonse of Spain. we have also heard that a Kaiser paid a visit, but we have not found this in print. Alf was also fond of telling the story of a 'marriage' in The Royal Oak. A man called Page decided that it was high time that a Mr King and his beloved (who were regular patrons of the pub) should get married. In fact he felt so strongly about it that he offered to perform the ceremony himself, for a payment of two gallons of bitter. The couple obviously decided that this was too good an offer to turn down, and Mr Page conducted the marriage with a towel tucked in his shirt collar. "They never had a ring so they just held hands" said Alf "and when it was over they went to live in Black Bush Cottage up on the hill and they was there for years an' they considered they were married".

The most famous of Alf's stories related to what happened at Midhurst Magistrates Court. Alf was in the process of renewing his licence for the pub when he was asked about the toilet facilities. His legendary reply was that he considered his facilities adequate enough and said: "But, sir, I have nine acres".

These days, the facilities are more modern. There is electric light and both internal and external toilets, but otherwise things have changed little. A good fire is still kept in the winter and in the spring the lawn blazes with a mass of daffodils. The only sad and surprising thing is that there is no memorial to this famous couple who kept The Royal Oak for all those years.

The Walk ....

From the Royal Oak car park climb back up the hill toward the main road. After climbing a fair way up the hill,

take the chalky right of way that is angled sharply back on the right. Avoid all deviations off this route until you are at a fork close to the white bungalow. Here, take the right-most route - the one without any gate or stile.

Continue on for a further 0.5 miles (0.8km), on a route that merrily winds its way, first descending into a valley, then starting to climb again. As you start this climb, you are faced with a fork in the routes, take the right-most lower route. Pass through the farm-yard of Buriton Farm and take the next opportunity to turn left, through (or round) a small six-bar wooden gate, onto the South Downs Way (SDW), that you are to follow to Harting Hill car park.

Initially our route on the SDW is 'fenced in'. As you enter the copse, continue on the SDW (the left route). After about 500 yards (457 metres), you will come upon a crossing of ways. Continue on the SDW taking the left-most of the two parallel routes to climb Pen Hill. As you start your descent from Pen Hill, you are faced with a decision on either deviating from the 'natural' route west which involves a steep scramble up Beacon Hill by the public bridleway, or alternatively follow the official route of the SDW. This diverts around the

hill, saving an ascent and descent of 160 feet (49 metres) but adding nearly a further mile (1.6km) to your walk. Assuming that you wish to enjoy the excellent views, climb Beacon Hill. From this point no further directions are necessary until you arrive at Harting Hill Car Park and Viewpoint, as you simply follow the South Downs Way signs and enjoy the views of Harting in the valley below.

As you pass the signboard indicating that you are leaving the Harting Down National Trust area, you will come to wooden gates. Take the bridleway (blue arrow) that turns left here. This bridleway heads toward the B2141 and although meandering in nature, runs roughly parallel to the road for about 0.5 miles (0.8km). You will come upon a public footpath from the road that crosses the bridleway. Turn left onto the footpath, passing through the wooden gate and walking along the right hand edge of the copse. You will pass through a wooden barrier to deter horseriding, and you then descend through the old yew wood to Bramshott Bottom.

At Bramshott Bottom, take the footpath opposite that runs diagonally and climbs Little Round Down. This is a pleasant climb on downland turf, and you pass little more than invasive hawthorn scrub and a solitary telephone wire. At the top you will meet the SDW where you should turn right. After approximately 700 yards (640 metres), you leave the SDW by

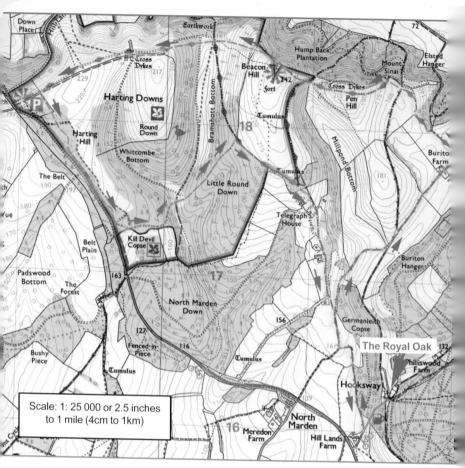

Scale: 1: 25 000 or 2.5 inches to 1 mile (4cm to 1km)

continuing straight on through the large wooden gates - the route becomes a public bridleway. The route around Telegraph House becomes metalled - part of the drive to the house. The drive is lined with a fine avenue of young beech trees. By the second white cottage, leave the tarmac drive, by passing through the small six-bar wooden gate and taking the footpath between enclosed fences. At the end of the path, climb the stile or use the gate to join the track that was your outgoing route. Follow this until you meet the narrow road to the Royal Oak, where you turn left to descend the hill back to the pub.

Pub File..........

The Royal Oak: Walkers are welcome and you can get your book 'pubberstamped' here. Opening times are 11.30am to 2.30pm and 6.30pm to 11pm on Tuesdays to Saturdays; and only from 11.30am to 2.30pm on Sundays. The pub is closed all day on Mondays. There is a restaurant, an extensive range of bar food and a daily 'Specials' board. Food is available during opening hours. The pub serves real ale. Children are welcome and are allowed into at least one area of the premises. Dogs are permitted if kept on a lead. The licensee is happy for walkers to park their cars in the car park providing they patronise the pub before or after their walk. (Tel: 01243 535257).

A CANAL MADE FAMOUS BY TURNER

(Where we walk the towpath, visit an old port, and discover a disused tram route)

Fact File.........

Starting Point: This walk starts from the Crown and Anchor at Dell Quay.

Alternative Parking and Start Point: There are a number of alternatives for parking around the route. There is a public car park just north of Hunston where the B2145 runs close to the canal and there is also one near St Mary's Church at Apuldram. Finally, there is a car park at the entrance to the marina. All of these car parks provide alternative start points for your walk.

Distance: Allow a little over 3 hours for this walk. The distance is 6.6 miles (10.6km).

Classification: 'Gentle'.

Safety and Comfort: Take care on the short stretch of road after St Mary's Church as there is no pavement and traffic travels fast here.

Maps: Ordnance Survey Landranger 1: 50 000 Series - Sheet 197.

Ordnance Survey Explorer 1: 25 000 Series - Sheet 120.

Ordnance Survey Pathfinder 1: 25 000 Series - Sheet 1305 (SU 80/90).

Map reference of start and finish - SU 835028.

Other Refreshment Possibilities: The Spinnaker Bar and Restaurant at Chichester Marina.

Travel by Car: Take the A27 from Portsmouth and then the A286. After just over a mile, turn right for Dell Quay.

Public Transport: Although Dell Quay is not directly served by a bus service, the nearby A286 that forms a short part of this walk is on a bus route. It is served every 20 minutes by Stagecoach Busline Service No 52/53 from Chichester (Tel: 01903 237661 for further information.

Background ....

We have always liked canal walks and in this part of the world there are few canals so opportunities are limited. The best time for this walk is in May when the canal banks are bright with spring flowers, but necessity forced us to walk the route in stormy December and even then it provided us with a memorable moment. Not far from the Chichester end of the canal, we were lucky enough to see a kingfisher. It is impossible to mistake the kingfisher for any other bird due to its bright iridescent blue/green colouring - a truly unforgettable and beautiful sight.

The walk is also full of historical interest, and starts at Dell Quay. This small port was built by the Lord Fitzwilliams of Cowdray in the late 15th and early 16th centuries. The port was prosperous into Tudor times, but suffered by its distance from Chichester, its lack of facilities and

St Mary's Church, Apuldram

was a spur running to Chichester, and the lower east/west section was part of the main canal. The junction was at Hunston. The bridges (originally swing bridges) have interesting names and one of the tasks of the Give-me-Five Treasure Hunt is to find out why they were named this way. Moving further west, the canal was in the form of a dredged channel around Thorney Island and Hayling Island. The final stage was the Portsea Canal from the east of Portsea Island to the west, although this was later superseded in 1830 by the cutting of a route around the north of Portsea Island to Portsmouth Harbour.

The canal suffered from being unable to compete with coasters for cost or speed. Canal traffic did not flow on the P&A after 1838 and it was formally abandoned in 1896. The Chichester Canal is perhaps now most famous as the subject of a J M W Turner painting of 1822, featuring a large brig in the foreground and the cathedral in the background. Since we last walked the canal several years ago, considerable progress has been made with its restoration and there are now very good information boards at each site where a bridge once stood.

The canal was once crossed via a drawbridge by the Selsey Tramway, which provided transportation for people and goods between Chichester and Selsey between 1897 - 1935.

silting up. It has been used over the years for many commodities, and in most recent times, coal cattle fodder and fertiliser were the most common. Nowadays, its purpose as a port has finished, but it is probably busier than ever with visiting yachtsman and tourists.

The Chichester Canal, designed by John Rennie, was part of the Portsmouth and Arundel (P&A) Canal, which in turn was part of a larger plan, that included the Thames, the Wey, the Arun Navigation and the Wey and Arun Canal, to link London and Portsmouth.

The P&A was opened in 1823, but like many canals, it was doomed to failure. At its peak it only carried 3,650 tons per year, compared with the 55,000 hoped for. The P and A left the Arun between Arundel and Littlehampton and headed west to meet the Chichester Channel at Salterns Lock. The uppermost (north/south) part of our walk along the canal

Give-me-Five Treasure Hunt
1. What was the main trade at Dell Quay in the 1700s?
2. What is the bird with red legs that can often be seen in Chichester Harbour?
3. What is the bird with a red breast that can often be seen in Chichester Harbour?
4. Which ship is mentioned in St Mary's churchyard?
5. The bridges over the Chichester Canal are named after people. Who were these people?

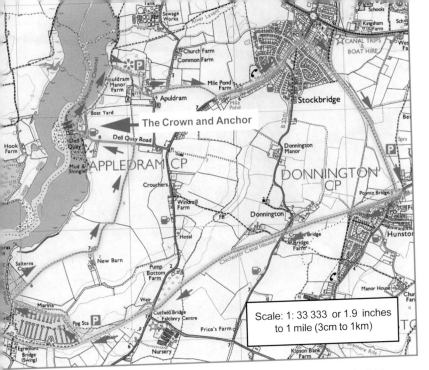

The Walk ....

This walk starts from the Crown and Anchor at Dell Quay. Proceed from the pub to the quay and turn right. Follow the path round and alongside the quay, at times it turns inward for a few steps and is generally undulating and uneven. After a distance of approximately 0.5 miles (0.8km) negotiate a wooden V-barrier, and pass the end of an old sunken trackway that is tree-covered. Turn right immediately after this, as directed by the fingerpost sign and after a few paces you pass through a small kissing gate. The church of St. Mary the Virgin at Apuldram is now ahead of you. Follow the right hand side of this field and then go through the churchyard.

Leave the churchyard by turning right through the gate by the main entrance to the church and walk along the pathway with the barbed wire fence on the right. At the end of this path, join the drive to swing left and then join the road at its corner by swinging left. Walk for about 250 yards (229 metres) in the direction of Fishbourne and Chichester. Be careful when walking this road, as traffic approaches quickly round the corner. Leave the road by turning right at the green metal fingerpost sign.

Walk along the path for some considerable distance with a ditch on your left and an open field on the right. In places this footpath is uneven so take care not to twist your ankle. At the end of the path you meet the A286 road. Turn left here and walk along the pavement on the right-hand side. After a short distance you pass a pond, carry on for about 0.7 miles (1.1km) passing the Selsey Tram pub on the right. Approximately 200 yards (183 km) after the turning signed to St. Wilfrid's Hospice, take a footpath off to the right opposite the post office and marked "Public Footpath - Selsey Tramway".

The path is initially a narrow tree

Storm clouds at Dell Quay

blocked off, the latter part being completely overgrown. At this point, the towpath is not surfaced and becomes softer going. Cross over Cutfield Bridge and resume your walk along the right-hand edge of the Canal. Soon you meet the road that takes you down to the Chichester Marina. After 0.5 miles (0.8km) you will come to the marina entrance, where you should bear right onto the road that runs along the right-hand side of the marina. Where the road meets the water's edge turn right onto the public footpath that runs along the right hand edge of Salterns Copse.

lined alley and you will cross a road that is part of a new housing estate. After about 400 yards (366 metres) on this path, you will have to pick your point to turn left through the trees and drop down onto the canal tow-path, to continue onward in the same direction. Although you are very low at this point and views are necessarily limited to those of the canal, it is nevertheless a very picturesque and tranquil scene. Walk along the towpath and cross over the Canal at Poyntz Bridge where you meet the B2145. Turn right for about 100 yards (91 metres) and then rejoin the Canal towpath, this time on the left of the Canal.

This section of the Canal is overgrown in various degrees with reeds and water lilies. When you get to Crosbie Bridge the Canal itself is

Leave the Copse walking along the surfaced footpath that runs between the two fields. The footpath then becomes a track and you head for New Barn. By the farm buildings and the oak tree you will meet a fully surfaced lane which you join, continuing to walk in approximately the same direction. Follow this lane and turn left onto the road that leads back to Dell Quay.

Pub File..........

The Crown and Anchor: Walkers are welcome and you can get your book 'pubberstamped' here. Opening times are 11am to 11pm on Mondays to Saturdays; midday to 10.30pm on Sundays. There is a restaurant, an extensive range of bar food and a daily 'Specials' board. Food is available from midday to 9.30pm on Mondays to Saturdays; midday to 9pm on Sundays. The pub serves real ale. Children are welcome and are allowed into at least one area of the pub. Dogs are permitted if kept on a lead. The licensee is happy for walkers to park their cars in the car park providing they patronise the pub before or after their walk. (Tel: 01243 781712)

A SHORT INVIGORATING WALK FROM COCKING

(An ideal short morning walk to follow a late night)

Fact File..........

Starting Point: This walk starts at the Blue Bell at Cocking.
Alternative Parking and Start Point: The walk can be started from the car park at Hilltop on the A286. This is shown as (P) on the map and is only a short distance from the route.
Distance: Allow just under 2 hours for this walk, the distance is 3.8 miles (6.1km).
Classification: 'Moderate' - the only climb consists of a simple ascent of the downs.
Safety and Comfort: No problems.
Maps: Ordnance Survey Landranger 1: 50 000 Series - Sheet 197.
Ordnance Survey Explorer 1: 25 000 Series - Sheet 120.
Ordnance Survey Pathfinder 1: 25 000 Series - Sheet 1286 (SU81/91).
Map reference of start and finish - SU 878176.
Other Refreshments Possibilities: There is a small restaurant in Cocking.
Travel by Car: The Blue Bell lies on the main A286 between Chichester and Midhurst.
Public Transport: Stagecoach Coastline Service No. 60 serves Cocking from Chichester or Midhurst. This is an hourly service, but does not run on Sundays (Tel: 01903 237661) for more information.

Background ....

There are, it seems, two ways of pronouncing the name of this village. Some time ago, we heard of an incident when a rather well-to-do resident of the area was asked for directions to the village. This dear old lady denied that the place existed until, when pressed, she eventually said "Oh you mean Kowing" (pronounced as if rhymed with towing).

Cocking is on a very busy road but is surprisingly unspoilt. It is unfortunate that although you

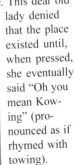

The Blue Bell, Cocking

Happy walkers near Cocking

Give-me-Five Treasure Hunt

This is a real test of how observant you are. Shown below are 5 views of small sections of wall that you will see around the route (not in order). All you have to do is spot them and tell us where they are by providing a 6-figure grid reference of their location.

experience the best of the downs on this walk, you only see a part of the village. As it is a short walk, you should have time to visit the church and stream, on the other side of the main road, so loved by W.H. Hudson the naturalist writer and praised in his 'Nature in Downland'. He wrote: "Cocking is one of many singularly interesting villages that nestle, half-hidden, in the shelter of the downs on the northern edge of the range. Out of a wooded coombe in the side of the sheltering hill issues a stream, and where it flows or trickles past the village it spreads out and forms a marsh grown over with tall reed and flowering rush, in summer blue with water forget-me-knot and water-mint. At the side of this blossoming marsh, in the middle of the green churchyard, sheltered and concealed by ancient trees, stands the small old church, one of the prettiest to be seen in the district. This beautiful church is situated at the edge of the village, on high ground behind the stream." The church was originally built for the Benedictines and the tower and south aisle were added to the Norman nave in the fourteenth century. The church has three medieval bells over 600 years old.

Striding it out on the South Downs Way

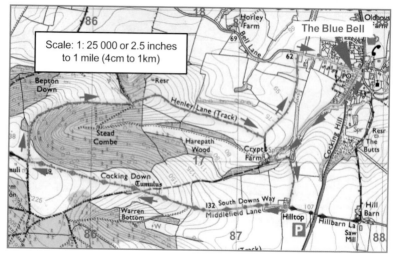

Scale: 1: 25 000 or 2.5 inches to 1 mile (4cm to 1km)

The Walk ....

From the Blue Bell, walk south along the A286 through the village. At the point where the main road swings to the left take the lane marked as a 'no through road' on the right and continue to follow this - you will be accompanied by a chalk stream below on your left. Pass under the railway arch and when you come to Crypt Farm, take the public right of way off to the left.

This is a chalky track that winds uphill between high hedgerows. You will arrive at the South Downs Way (SDW) where you should turn right.

Your route follows the SDW for a little over 1 mile (1.6km). After about 0.7 miles (1.1km), a bridleway will cross the way in diagonal fashion - ignore this and turn right at the next right of way about 0.5 miles (0.8km) later.

Follow this byway gently downhill with the yew-wooded slopes of Stead Combe on your right. After 0.6 miles (1km), avoid the left turn that descends steeply down the chalky track, and continue straight on. You will find yourself at a junction of ways close to Crypt Farm. Turn left here, and walk between high hedgerows, eventually joining a concrete track to meet the road.

Turn right and walk for a short distance back to the Blue Bell.

Pub File..........

The Blue Bell Inn: Walkers are welcome and you can get your book 'pubberstamped' here. Opening times are midday to 11pm on Mondays to Saturdays; midday to 10.30pm on Sundays. The restaurant menu, 'A Taste in the Country' includes Wild Boar, Venison, Pheasant, Kangaroo, Ostrich and even Crocodile! There is an extensive range of bar food and a daily 'Specials' board. Food is available all day, every day. There are three real ales on offer, Greene King IPA, Abbot and Bass. Children are very welcome in two areas of the pub. Dogs are permitted if kept on a lead. The licensee is happy for walkers to park their cars in the car park providing they patronise the pub before or after their walk. (Tel: 01730 813449).

GLORIOUS GOODWOOD

(And where you may also see a free fox)

Fact File..........

Starting Point: This walk starts from the Fox Goes Free in the village of Charlton, West Sussex.

Alternative Parking and Start Point: Alternative start points are the car parks at The Harroways near Goodwood Race Course and at The Triangle, both shown as (P) on the map.

Distance: Allow 2 hours 20 minutes for this walk, the distance is 4.6 miles (7.4km).

Classification: 'Moderate'.

Safety and Comfort: No problems.

Maps: Ordnance Survey Landranger 1: 50 000 Series - Sheet 197.

Ordnance Survey Explorer 1: 25 000 Series - Sheet 120.

Ordnance Survey Pathfinder 1: 25 000 Series - Sheet 1286 (SU 81/91).

Map reference of start and finish - SU 889130.

Other Refreshment Possibilities: A slight deviation from the route will take you to Singleton where there is a tea room and the Horse and Groom.

Travel by Car: From Chichester, take the Midhurst road (A286) to Singleton and then take a right turn to Charlton which is about 1 mile (1.6 km) due east of Singleton.

Public Transport: Travel by bus to Charlton is not really feasible as the service is restricted to Wednesdays and Saturdays with one journey only. However, if you start the walk from Singleton, you can get there easily by using the Stagecoach Coastline Service No. 60 from Chichester or Midhurst. This is an hourly service, but does not run on Sundays (Tel: 01903 237661) for more information.

Background ....

There has been racing at Goodwood since 1801, when it was started by the third Duke of Richmond, the course originally being known as The Harroways. Race-goers often used to arrive by train to the old Singleton Station and then proceeded by carriage up to the course. Goodwood was very popular at the time of Edward VII who loved the event and described it as being "a garden party with racing tacked on".

This is not only a horseracing area but also foxhunting country, and the pub from which we start has been known as The Fox or a similar name for at least as far back as 1750. Over recent years it has gone from The Fox, to The Fox Goes Free, then The

The Fox Goes Free

Charlton Fox and a short time ago back to The Fox Goes Free. Depending on who you talk to, the name either records a reversion of the pub to a free house, or the more romantic notion that the name is taken from the legend that Sussex foxes, by working in packs, completely bewildered the local Charlton Hunt. Between 1670 and 1750, the Charlton Hunt was one of the most prominent in England and included, either as members or visitors, King William III, the Grand Duke of Tuscany and many other dukes, earls and barons. They usually stayed nearby and no doubt drank at the pub which at that time was known as the Pig and Whistle. There is a famous manuscript that lays claim that the Charlton Hunt was superior to all others, due to the epic chase that took place on Friday 26th January 1738. The manuscript takes two pages to describe a struggle that started in the morning at East Dean Woods and finished ten hours and ten miles (16 km) away at South Stoke - a village near the River Arun. Here the 23 hounds killed an old vixen having chased her back and forth between Cocking, Westdean Forest, Graffham, Cowdray Park, Goodwood, Halnaker Hill, Eartham Common, Slindon Down and Houghton. A further claim to fame of the Charlton Fox is that it was the meeting place of the first ever Women's Institute group in England in 1915.

Give-me-Five Treasure Hunt

Shown below are five pictures taken in order around the route. Just keep alert and you will see the items as you walk. All you need to do is to tell us what they are and where you found them.

The Walk ....

Proceed up the lane to pass the phone box on your left. Bear left as directed on the public bridleway and the route becomes a shingly track.

Proceed up the hill - there is an imposing red-brick house on the left and a saw mill on the right. Pass under the power lines and there is now a pleasant gentle climb along a shaded sunken bridleway. There is a beautifully positioned seat alongside the route half way up that is a perfect place to stop, relax and enjoy the view

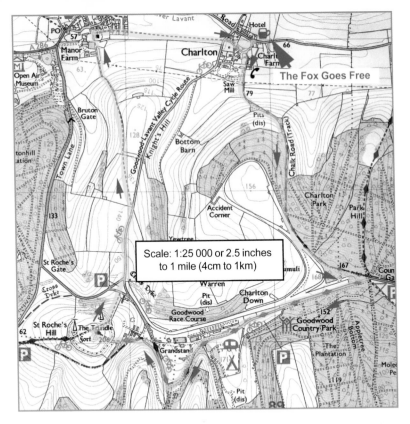

Scale: 1:25 000 or 2.5 inches to 1 mile (4cm to 1km)

if you have the time. As the bridleway arrives at the top of the hill, you will see the white rails of the racecourse, and you should continue with these accompanying you on your right. The bridleway widens and then you meet the road on a sharp bend where you turn right.

This road takes you almost due west with Goodwood Country Park on the left and the racecourse immediately on your right. Having passed the grandstand the road veers to the left. Continue following the road, and then at the T-junction turn right in the direction of Singleton and Midhurst. Follow the roadside for approximately 300 yards (274 metres) - take care as it is a busy road - and then turn left as directed by the public bridleway sign. After a few yards, turn off left through the beech trees to continue following the public bridleway and then climb the steep hill.

After a few yards, you will turn right onto a signposted public footpath - be careful, it is easy to miss - and climb St Roches Hill with the iron railings on your right. Pass through the swing gate, over the ridges of the earthwork, and onward toward the Triangulation Point. Here at the

A glorious view from the Trundle

Towards Singleton

Trundle on top of St. Roches Hill, is the climax of the walk. From this height of 676 feet (206 metres) you can literally see for miles in all directions.

Having enjoyed the views, turn right at the triangulation point to follow the grassy path, walk through the gap in the earthworks and then downhill to the Triangle Car Park. Cross the main road and take the narrow road towards Charlton, and follow it for about 700 yards (640 metres). Take the footpath to the left that leaves the road by a stile, and only gradually diverges from the line of the road. At the time of writing, this footpath was well-marked by a line of posts. Carry on down the hill with the fence on your right, towards the stile at the bottom. Follow the farm track for a short distance to a further stile, then cross the farmyard to enter the churchyard through the gate.

Walk along the edge of the churchyard to the further gate in the corner, and then turn right to continue with the low churchyard wall on the left and high hedge on the right. Keep going in the same easterly direction and your route now takes you through some pleasant terraced houses and you then (rather unusually) walk through the covered walkway to 'House No.1'. You will now find yourself in a small estate of older houses - pick up the narrow footpath between the box hedges and after about 30 yards (27 metres) pass through the small swing gate into the field.

The footpath then heads easterly through this field with the Singleton to Charlton road running parallel about 200 yards (183 metres) away on the left. The footpath emerges at a stile, opposite some terraced flint cottages. Walk along the lane opposite, accompanied by attractive cottages on either side and after about 200 yards (183 metres) you will find that you are at the war memorial, where you turn left and re-trace your steps back to the Fox Goes Free.

Pub File.........

Walkers are welcome and you can get your book 'pubberstamped' here. Opening times for are 11am to 3pm and 6pm to 11pm on Mondays to Saturdays; midday to 4pm and 7pm to 10.30pm on Sundays. There is a restaurant, a wide range of bar food and sometimes there is a 'Specials' board. Food is available every day from midday to 2.30pm and 6.30pm to 10.30pm. The pub serves real ale. Children are welcome and are allowed into at least one area of the premises. Dogs are permitted if kept on a lead. Some overnight accommodation is available. The licensee is happy for walkers to park their cars in the car park providing they patronise the pub before or after their walk. (Tel: 01243 811461).

THE OLD STRAIGHT ROAD

(Where we learn the proper way to build roads and a little bit about a childrens' poet)

Fact File..........

Starting Point: This walk starts from the George at Eartham
Alternative Parking and Start Point: If you are not parking at the pub, the roads in parts of the village are wide enough for parking, although please park tidily so as not to cause a nuisance. This walk can also be started from the car park at Eartham Wood - see map.
Distance: Allow 3 hours for the walk, the distance is 6.2 miles (10 km).
Classification: 'Could make you puff' - there are no particularly demanding hills on this route, but there are several moderate climbs.
Safety and Comfort: You should take care at the very beginning and end of this walk, as you have to walk on the main road through the village and this has poor visibility.
Maps: Ordnance Survey Landranger 1: 50 000 Series - Sheet 197.
Ordnance Survey Explorer 1: 25 000 Series - Sheet 121.
Ordnance Survey Pathfinder 1: 25 000 Series - Sheets 1286 (SU 81/91) and 1305 (SU 80/90).
Map reference of start and finish - SU 939095.
Other Refreshment Possibilities: None.
Travel by Car: From Chichester take the A285 to just beyond Halnaker. Turn off right where indicated to Eartham and keep following signs for the village.
Public Transport: Travel by bus is not feasible.

Background ....

Stane Street is thought to have been constructed by Belinus - a Roman engineer. Billingshurst (originally a wood that had to be penetrated by Stane Street) and Billingsgate (the point where Stane Street entered London) may have both been named after him. The road ran between London (Londinium) and Chichester (Regnum) and is a southerly continuation of Ermine Street. Much of the road remains in use today. The present A3 and A24 through South London via Tooting and Merton follow the original alignment, as does the A29 between Dorking and Pulborough. Southwest of our walk, Stane Street enters Chichester on the route of the present day A285.

A popular misconception is that all Roman Roads are straight. Certainly, individual sections are straight and their roads were made as direct as possible, but advantage was also taken of individual geographical features. For example: Stane Street deviates from a straight line to pass through the Mole Gap at Dorking, where the Rive Mole passes through the North Downs. Further southwest (slightly northeast of our walk) the route again deviates slightly, to make use of a convenient spur to the north of Bignor Hill. The Romans also made use of existing tracks if they were the best

The six-way junction on Stane Street

and most natural routes.

As we all know the roads lasted for hundreds of years; in some cases to the present day. What techniques led to this superb durability? The first step was to dig out a trench, with a ditch on either side for drainage. Then, a foundation of big stones or flints was carefully laid at the bottom of the trench. Next, came several layers of rammed chalk and gravel. On the best roads, the top surface was made of stone slabs, cemented together in a raised curve to help surface water run off. On lesser roads the surface was made of gravel. To sum up then, the secret of the roads was their drainage. The cambered surface and ditches meant that they were exceedingly well drained and water did not collect on them.

Stane Street, in particular, was built around 70 AD. It was metalled, cambered and 20-25 feet (6.1-7.6 metres) wide in places. It was built on an embankment (agger), with side ditches 85 feet (25.9 metres) apart. In many places the camber is still very evident. The side ditches are also visible in places.

On this walk we also pass Courthill Farm, which was rented for a short time by the writer Hilaire Belloc in 1905. He stayed there with his wife Elodie and five children while they looked for their dream home, which they found eventually at Kings Land, Shipley. Belloc produced an extraordinary volume of work during his working career between 1899 to 1942 that covered a wide and diverse range of subjects: children's poems and verse, essays, historical works, novels, travel and sailing books. He was also an MP for a short period before becoming disenchanted with politics.

He was an undoubted romantic and a love of Sussex is a common thread throughout his work. As his life progressed he became increasingly concerned that the old Sussex countryside and its dialect and ways were disappearing as London bore down from the north. Hilaire Belloc died at Shipley in 1953.

The Walk ....

With your back to the George, turn right and follow the main road with Great Ballard School on your right. Take great care as there is no pavement or verge. After about 200 yards (183 metres), (where the road swings sharp right) turn left and walk along the track (public footpath). You will see a track off to the left at about 0.6 miles (1km), avoid this and continue to follow the public footpath indicated by the yellow arrows. The path then follows two sides of a field and in the far corner you will find a stile.

Climb this to turn left to follow the pleasant shaded bridleway. You will climb steadily and after just over 0.5 miles (0.8km) arrive at a more open area. After about 200 yards (183 metres) in this less heavily-wooded section you will meet a further bridleway (unsigned at the time of walking) where you should turn left onto a chalky track that descends rapidly. A little over 500 yards (457 metres) later you will come to a further junction of bridleways (there will be a barrier in front of you) and here you should turn left.

Give-me-Five Treasure Hunt

This is a tree hunt. There are five specimens that we photographed around the route for you to find. We have tried to pick out trees with a characteristic shape, or include a distinctive object in the picture to help you find the specimen. All you have to do is write down where you find them (distance in miles from the start) and what type of tree they are. Use the scale map provided to measure off the distance from the start to the object. (Young children will need some parental assistance for this).

Follow this bridleway with its blue arrows, along the edge of the wood and you will eventually pass through a swing barrier at the Forestry Commission Offices and Store Sheds. Walk past another barrier to the road. Turn right onto the road for about 70 yards (64 metres) and then turn right alongside a wooden barrier to pick up the inauspicious bridleway that is Stane Street. Continue along this straight track for just under 1 mile (1.6km) until you arrive at the six-way crossing. Turn right here to leave Stane Street (signposted to Slindon).

After 0.6 miles (1km) carry straight on at a crossing of bridleways and continue for a similar distance until you emerge from Northwood onto a surfaced but very narrow lane where you should turn right. Just after passing Courthill Farm, turn right onto the wide track that is a public footpath. You will negotiate one gate/ stile combination and just after the track swings sharply right, climb the stile to leave the track to follow the left side of a large field. Climb the

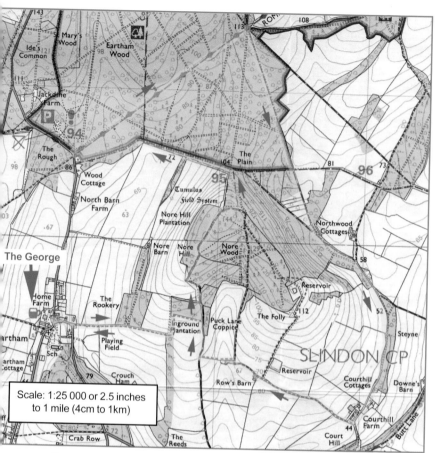

Scale: 1:25 000 or 2.5 inches to 1 mile (4cm to 1km)

stile at the end of the field, and turn right onto the shaded bridleway. After about 400 yards (366 metres), leave the bridleway by climbing the bank and stile. You will realise that you have now met your outgoing route, and you should re-trace your steps back to The George.

Pub File..........

The George: Walkers are welcome and you can get your book 'pubberstamped' here. Opening times are 11am to 3pm and 6pm to 11pm on Mondays to Saturdays; midday to 3pm and 7pm to 10.30pm on Sundays. There is a restaurant, a range of bar food is available and there is a daily 'Specials' board. Food is available from midday to 2pm and 6.30pm to 9pm on Mondays to Thursdays; midday to 2pm and 6.30pm to 9.30pm on Fridays and Saturdays and from midday to 2pm on Sundays. No food is available on Sunday evenings. The pub serves real ale. Children are welcome and are allowed into at least one area of the premises. Dogs are permitted if kept on a lead. The licensee is happy for walkers to park their cars in the car park providing they patronise the pub before or after their walk. (Tel: 01243 814340).

A ROYAL WALK

(Where we follow the Arun and climb up to the high downs for some magnificent views)

Fact File.........

Starting Point: This walk starts from the George and Dragon at Houghton (near Amberley, West Sussex).

Alternative Parking and Start Point: If you do not use the George and Dragon's Car Park, then park where we did (shown on the map).

Distance: Allow just over 3 hours for this walk - the distance is 6.4 miles (10.3km).

Classification: 'Could make you puff' - most of the walk is flat, but there is a stiff climb from West Burton village to the top of West Burton Hill.

Safety and Comfort: It is necessary to cross the A29 in two places - take care here - although the visibility is good, it is a very fast road. From the comfort viewpoint, the initial section on the river bank appears to lay wet at most times of the year, so waterproof footwear is important for this walk.

Maps: Ordnance Survey Landranger 1: 50 000 Series - Sheet 197.
Ordnance Survey Explorer 1: 25 000 Series - Sheet 121.
Ordnance Survey Pathfinder 1: 25 000 Series - Sheet 1286 (SU 81/91) and 1287 (TQ 01/11).
Map reference of start and finish - SU 017115.

Other Refreshment Possibilities: At 2.7 miles (4.3km) there is the Squire and House pub (where you cross the A29 after passing through Bury).

Travel by Car: Houghton is approached from the A29 Chichester to London Road and then the B2139 road to Storrington.

Public Transport: Houghton is served by a limited community bus service that runs between Chichester and Worthing. Nearby Amberley is served by Service 73 from Horsham. (Tel: 0345 959099 West Sussex Travel Line for further information). Amberley also has a railway station (Tel: 0345 484950 for train times).

Background ....

It seems almost mandatory that for an old pub to be worth its salt, it must have had a royal visitor. And so it is with The George and Dragon, not only a royal visitor but Charles II no less, on his escape to France in 1651, after the Battle of Worcester. The best accounts say that he rested on the night of Monday, October 13, near Hambledon after meeting up with Colonel George Gunter of Racton, and

at daybreak journeyed by way of Broadhalfpenny Down (the birthplace of cricket), and then via Catherington Down, Chalton Down and Idsworth Down to Compton Down. Continuing over the hills and descending at Duncton Beacon, the party had a narrow escape in Houghton Forest where they nearly met Captain Morley, the governor of Arundel Castle.

The peaceful village of Bury

Their route then took them through Houghton and the King reputedly took ale at the inn and thus fortified, he crossed the Arun to Amberley where he slept at the castle. On the South Downs at Amberley Mount, the King's horse threw a shoe and this was repaired at Lee Farm at Barpham from where he rode onward to Brighton to reach Fecamp on 16 October. That is the story as the Amberley folk will tell it.

If you have time after your walk, Amberley is worth a visit. It has, of course, its Chalk Pits Museum next to the railway station. Here you will find (assuming it is unchanged from when we last visited it) displays of local crafts and industries including quarrying, lime burning and a working printer, a potter and a black-smith. The bridge that you cross to get to Amberley is very old, like many on the Arun and West Rother and was restored by the bishops of Chichester in the fifteenth century. One of the great painters of Sussex scenes lived at Amberley in a beautiful thatched cottage in the village itself. Edward Stott showed, as so eloquently put by E.V. Lucas, "how the clear skin of a Sussex boy takes the light, and how the Southdown sheep drink at hill ponds beneath a violet sky, and that there is nothing more beautiful under the stars than a whitewashed cottage just when the lamp is lit". Close by is Amberley Wild Brooks; a wonderful name, conjuring up visions of winter-flooded fields, early morning mists and fowl everywhere. An often quoted story is that when an Amberley

Give-me-Five Treasure Hunt

For this walk we have derived a cottage hunt. You will need to be very observant for this one. The task is to find the names of five cottages on the route that are connected with the following:

1. *A river*
2. *A religious feast (although you may find the spelling unusual).*
3. *A sweet scented plant.*
4. *An insect.*
5. *A saint.*

*King Charles II
woz here as well*

resident is asked where they live; in the summer they answer, "Amberley, where else would you live?", and in the winter - "Amberley, God help us", such is the wetness of the place.

The beautiful villages alongside the Arun also require a mention; Offham, South Stoke and Bury - a hamlet that once had the little boat ferry to Amberley, but which is now sadly defunct. On a fine summer day the Arun Valley and the surrounding downland is one of the most beautiful places in England. We have no doubt that this walk will provide you with a most memorable day.

The Walk ....

From the George and Dragon Car Park, turn left onto the B2139 and walk down the road and turn right into South Lane. The lane is lined by beautiful thatched cottages - continue to the very end of this little lane, pass through the metal swing gate and turn half right onto the bridleway. Walk for about 100 yards (91 metres) and then turn left toward the river and then walk left (east) to follow the river bank.

The Arun is tidal here and stays so until beyond Pulborough. Although this means a less attractive river, it gives a pleasing extra dimension to our walk supplying the sight and calls of estuarine birds in addition to an already attractive habitat that provides the ghostly grey heron, lapwing and normal lowland birds. This habitat coupled with the downs rising steeply away on two sides provides one of the

most beautiful and varied areas of countryside in the south country.

Initially this footpath is boggy and examining the winter undergrowth it looks as if it could provide a jolly good crop of stinging nettles in the summer months - our fingers are crossed for you! Continue to follow the river bank, crossing the odd small footbridge and stile, until you come to the stile at the immediate left of the old Amberley Bridge. Carefully cross the road here, climb the stile on the other side to rejoin the river bank to continue your progress along the Arun. Enjoyment of this peaceful pastoral environment is somewhat enhanced by the sight and sound of the distant traffic that can be seen scurrying back and forth, on the roads high up in the hills around you.

Our route meanders, following the river towards Bury. As you near Bury you will pass through two gates and two stiles and when almost alongside the church, bear half left leading to a lane that takes you past the church of St John the Evangelist and up through Bury. Continue on this lane over the crossroads, passing the one-time house of novelist John Galsworthy of Forsyte Saga fame (where he spent the last seven years of his life), and on until you meet the A29.

Cross the main road very carefully and proceed along Westburton Lane. This is a very quiet lane, ignoring all turnings (including those to Bignor) for 0.5 mile (0.8km) until you reach the house called Fogdens, where you take the bridleway to the left. This is a pleasant leafy way whose incline gradually increases. When at the top of the hill, by the three black barns, turn left and follow the South Downs Way. Little direction is required here, just follow the South Downs Way over

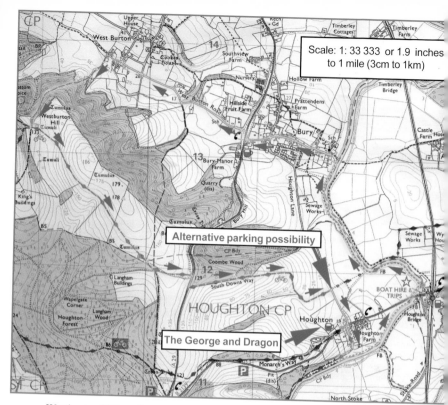

Westburton Hill until you again reach the A29. Turn right and follow the A29 for a few yards until you have to cross (very carefully) and rejoin the South Downs Way. If ever a view called for a wide-angle camera lens to capture the full magnitude of its beauty, this is one - the Arun lying as a sleepy snake below, the South Downs and the quarry at Amberley to the right, and further right the hills of Arundel Park.

Follow the chalky South Downs Way down toward the minor country road below - you will no doubt spot The George and Dragon in the distance at this point. At the road, turn right and climb the hill that takes you back to the village of Houghton. At the B2139 turn right for a few yards to return to The George and Dragon.

Pub File..........

The George and Dragon: Walkers are welcome and you can get your book 'pubberstamped' here. Opening times are 11am to 3pm and 6pm to 11pm on Mondays to Fridays; 11am to 11pm on Saturdays; midday to 10.30pm on Sundays. There is a restaurant, an extensive range of bar food and a daily 'Specials' board. Food is available from midday to 2.30pm and 6pm to 9.30pm on Mondays to Fridays; midday to 10.00pm on Saturdays; and midday to 9.30pm on Sundays. The pub serves real ale. Children are welcome and are allowed into at least one area of the premises. Dogs are permitted if kept on a lead. The licensee is happy for walkers to park their cars in the car park providing they patronise the pub before or after their walk, but as space is limited it would be much appreciated if cars could be parked carefully. (Tel: 01793 831559).

THE ITCHEN VALLEY

(Where we meander pleasantly along the River Itchen almost to its source)

Fact File..........

Starting Point: This ride starts from the Cricketers Inn at Easton near Winchester.

Alternative Parking and Start Point: If you do not wish to park at the Cricketers Inn, you can utilise the public car park at Avington and start the ride from there.

Distance: Allow 2 hours 30 minutes for this ride, the return distance to Cheriton and back is 14.4 miles (23.2km). If you start from the alternative car park at Avington, a return distance of 12.8 miles (20.6km) is obtained.

Surface and Nature of Route: This ride follows very quiet country lanes through the villages of the Itchen Valley.

Classification: 'Gentle' - there are no significant hills on this ride.

Safety and Comfort: No problems.

Maps: Ordnance Survey Landranger 1: 50 000 Series - Sheet 185.

Map reference of start and finish - SU 511321.

Local Cycle Hire: Somborne Cycles, 3 Nutcher's Drove, King's Somborne, Hants SO20 6PA (Tel: 01794 388327).

Other Refreshments on the Ride: In Easton, in addition to the Cricketers Inn, there is the Chestnut Horse. In Ovington at 4 miles (6.4km) there is the Bush Inn; in Tichborne at 5 miles (8km) there is the Tichborne Arms, and after 8 miles (12.9km) in Cheriton there is the Flower Pots Inn.

Travel by Car: Easton lies 2 miles (3.2km) north east of Winchester, and is approached either from the A31 or the B3047.

Background ....

Although this ride is one of the furthest from Portsmouth, it is in our view the best ride in the book. We start from the delightful village of Easton, and follow the course of the River Itchen almost to its source at Cheriton. We always like to take advantage of the course of a river when walking or cycling, as it offers a route without steep hills. Often on a walk this is not easy, as over the course of time, fishing rights usually seem to have taken precedence over pedestrian rights, and it is very rare to find a

Avington House

footpath along a river bank. With cycling it is easier, as there is often a main road, and with luck a parallel back road quietly running through the river valley. In this ride, we follow the quietest of back roads that it is possible to find in Hampshire. There are also plenty of opportunities to picnic alongside the crystal-clear River Itchen, or if you prefer it you can stop at one of the several pubs, conveniently placed along the route. This is a linear ride, and directions are only given for the outward journey. To return, merely re-trace your route back to Easton.

Places to explore around the route ....

Tichborne: The name of the village and the family is thought to arise from "At Itchenbourne", due to the proximity of the rising of the River Itchen nearby in Cheriton. The village is well known for the old custom of the Tichborne Dole, which was provided as a result of a great deal of hard work by one particular lady. The dole originated in the reign of Henry I and arose as a result of a promise made by Sir Roger Tichborne to his dying and bedridden wife. She asked him if he would give some land to a charitable trust, and the cunning man promised to allocate as much land as she could drag herself around while a firebrand stayed alight. She heroically managed to encircle 8 hectares (20 acres), and the area is still known as "The Crawls". After this achievement, she encouraged the continuity of the dole, by placing a curse on the family if ever it was not distributed annually. This was continued until 1894 with the distribution of 2000 loaves, but because of unseemly scenes, money then replaced bread.

The Bush Inn at Ovington: We love old pubs and that is why we always enjoy a visit to the Bush Inn. They say that you often cannot tell a book by its cover, and that is the case with old country pubs. Inside there is an atmosphere of comfort and timelessness. There are huge salmon in cases and the walls are stained by the smoke of ages. It was built in the 17th century and is situated on the Pilgrims Way. The unspoilt nature of the pub has encouraged film producers to come on location here. The most famous visitors were Richard Burton and Sophia Loren who were here for the 1975 remake of Brief Encounter. But it is the position of the pub alongside one of the most attractive spots on the River Itchen that makes it such a wonderful place to visit. The river is at its most attractive here with a long footbridge and walks along the riverbank.

Cycle Ride Directions ....

A. 0.0 (0.0): From the Cricketers Inn, turn left (the road is signposted to "Avington 1½, Ovington 3½").

B. 1.1 (1.1): Pass into Avington Park.

C. 0.2 (1.3): At the Avington junction turn left to ride through Avington.

D. 0.5 (1.8): After you leave Avington village, at the point where the road swings sharp left in the direction of the lodge house, bear off right to cycle with the golf course on your right.

E. 1.8 (3.6): At the "give way" junction (no signpost) turn left to cycle down into Ovington and then after crossing the small bridge, turn right. (A left turn here would take you to the lovely old Bush Inn).

F. 0.8 (4.4): At the junction with the B3047 turn left as marked "Alresford 1½" - be careful as traffic is fast here - and just after the 40 mph sign turn right on the road signposted to Tichborne. It will probably be best to

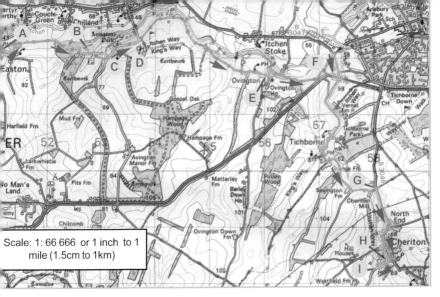

Scale: 1: 66 666 or 1 inch to 1 mile (1.5cm to 1km)

dismount and use the islands to cross the road.

G. 2.4 (6.8): After passing through Tichborne, and at the junction by the bus stop, turn right on the B3046 signposted to "Cheriton 1".

H. 0.7 (7.5): In Cheriton, just after passing the war memorial, turn right as directed to "Winchester 7, Bishops Waltham 7".

I. 0.2 (7.7): Arrive at the Flower Pots Inn and the Cheriton Brewhouse.

(No further directions are necessary as the return journey follows the same route as your outward journey).

The Cricketers at Easton

Pub File..........

The Cricketers Inn: Cyclists are welcome and you can get your book 'pubberstamped' here. Opening times are midday to 3pm and 6pm to 11pm on Mondays to Fridays; midday to 11pm on Saturdays and midday to 10.30pm on Sundays. There is a restaurant, an extensive range of bar food and a daily 'Specials' board. Food is available daily from midday to 2pm and 6pm to 9pm. The pub serves six different real ales from around the country. Children are welcome and are allowed into at least one area of the premises. Dogs are permitted if kept on a lead. Three rooms can be let for overnight accommodation. The licensee is happy for cyclists to park their cars in the car park providing they patronise the pub before or after their ride. (Tel: 01962 779353).

CYCLING THE MEON VALLEY

(Where we ride traffic-free on an old railway line for several miles)

Fact File..........

Starting Point: The Shoe Inn at Exton.

Alternative Parking and Start Point: An alternative place to park your car is at the point where you turn off the A32 for Exton, when approaching from the north - see map.

Distance: Allow 2 hours for this ride, the distance is 9.4 miles (15.1km).

Classification: 'Gentle' - an extremely level ride.

Surface and Nature of Route: The first half of this ride is on quiet lanes that run along the river valley. The return leg is via the Meon Valley Cycle Trail. Due to heavy usage by horse riders, it can be fairly soft and muddy.

Safety and Comfort: No problems.

Maps: Ordnance Survey Landranger 1: 50 000 Series - Sheets 185 and 196.

Map reference of start and finish - SU 612209.

Local Cycle Hire: Owens Cycles, Lavant Street, Petersfield (Tel: 01730 260446).

Other Refreshments on the Ride: You will pass the Hurdles at 2 and 8 miles (3.2 and 12.9km), White Lion at 3 miles (4.8km) and Bold Forester at 4.5 miles (7.2km).

Travel by Car: Exton lies just off the A32, south of Warnford.

Background ....

This ride starts from the Shoe Inn at Exton - a pub with a delightfully-placed garden that has the infant River Meon at its foot. The ride initially follows very quiet lanes from Exton down to Soberton Heath and then returns to Exton via a cycleway that follows the track of the disused Meon Valley Railway. If you have very young children, then you may wish to minimise the length of time that you spend on the roads and do a "there and back" on the old railway route. We last checked this route on a wet January day and at that time the poor old village of Exton was suffering badly with severe flooding due to the River Meon overflowing its banks, and by the end of the ride we were pretty wet. Thankfully, this is only an occasional occurrence and we are sure that you will enjoy this very pleasant ride.

Freedom on a spring morning

Places to explore around the route ....

The Meon Valley Railway: We cannot claim to be true railway enthusiasts, but like everyone that lived through the final days of steam, and the period before the Beeching branch line closures in the 1960s, we remember the old branch lines with great affection and a certain amount of nostalgia. It is also very pleasant to be able to take advantage of the flat and easy cycling that is obtained from following the line of an old railway route. The Meon Valley Line was opened in June 1903 and was operated by the London and South Western Railway (LSWR). Although the permanent way was constructed wide enough to take two tracks, only one was ever built. In the early days the line was busy and carried more goods than passenger traffic, one of the main commodities being market garden produce - including strawberries in season - for which the Meon Valley was famous. Significant amounts of coal, milk and livestock were also carried to the markets at Alton and Fareham. Trains became smaller and smaller, shrinking from 10 carriages to 2 in the 1920s. Competition from the commercial lorry also took its toll. The line limped on for 30 or so more years, but closure began in 1955 although some isolated sections carried on until 1968.

Soberton: Here you will see the old railway station. Although this is now a private house, it is still recognisable as an old LSWR design. The station's claim to fame, is that in the summer of 1944, Sir Winston Churchill spent some days making crucial decisions with his staff, immediately prior to the invasion of Europe on D Day, June 6th 1944. The party also contained Eisenhower, Smuts, Mackenzie King, de Gaulle, Eden and Bevin, and they were housed in the station and in eight red LMS coaches and an LNER sleeping car.

Alternative Parking

Scale: 1: 50 000 or 1.3 inches to 1 mile (2cm to 1km)

A pause for a photograph

Cycle Ride Directions ....

A. 0.0 (0.0): Leave the Shoe Inn car park, turn right, cross the river by the bridge and carefully cross the A32 into Stocks Lane, and take the first turning right opposite a property called Stocks Meadow.

B. 0.4 (0.4): At the end of Rectory Lane, swing right and left as signposted to "Droxford 1½, Soberton 2½".

C. 1.5 (1.9): When you meet the B2150, turn left to cross under the bridge carrying the cycle trail on which you will return, and turn right by the Hurdles pub into Station Road as signposted to "Soberton 1¼".

D. 1.0 (2.9): At the give-way junction by Soberton Parish Hall, turn right as directed to "Soberton Heath, Newtown and Southwick".

E. 0.8 (3.7): At Webbs Green, bear right down the hill into Selworth Lane as directed to "Soberton Heath, Swanmore and Bishops Waltham".

F. 0.1 (3.8): At the bottom of Selworth Lane, swing left to climb the hill as directed to "Soberton Heath, Newtown and Southwick".

G. 0.9 (4.7): After entering Soberton Heath, turn right and cycle along a narrow lane marked "no through road for motor vehicles".

H. 0.2 (4.9): When you come to the bridge over the Meon Valley Cycle Trail, drop down to the trail and head in a direction that takes you to the right (north).

I. 4.1 (9.0): Leave the cycle way at the point of the missing bridge near Shavards Farm, descend to the road, and at the grassy triangular junction, swing left to climb the hill back to Exton.

J. 0.2 (9.2): At the end of Stocks Lane, carefully cross the A32 into Beacon Hill Lane.

K. 0.2 (9.4): Arrive back at the Shoe Inn.

Pub File..........

The Shoe Inn: Cyclists are welcome and you can get your book 'pubberstamped' here. Opening times are 11am to 3pm and 6pm to 11pm on Mondays to Saturdays; midday to 3pm and 7pm to 10.30pm on Sundays. An extensive range of bar food is available and a daily 'Specials' board. Food is available from midday to 2pm and 7pm to approx. 9pm Mondays to Saturdays; and from midday to 2pm on Sundays. The pub serves real ale. Children are welcome and are allowed into at least one area of the premises. Dogs are permitted if kept on a lead. The licensee is happy for cyclists to park their cars in the car park providing they patronise the pub before or after their ride. (Tel: 01489 877526).

A VISIT TO THE BAT AND BALL
(Where we climb to the nursery of cricket)

Fact File..........

Starting Point: The Travellers Rest at Newtown.
Alternative Parking and Start Point: There is a Forestry Commission Car Park at Forest Walk near Denmead (see map).
Distance: Allow 2 hours 10 minutes for this ride - the distance is 13 miles (20.9km).
Surface and Nature of Route: The majority of this ride takes place over some delightfully quiet country lanes and at times it is a surprise to see a car. Some care is needed at the beginning and end of the route, between Points A and C and U and V, as these are straight roads and inevitably traffic travels fast.
Classification: 'Moderate' - you would not expect to visit Broadhalfpenny Down without a climb or two, but fortunately, the ascent is gradual and it is only when you descend into Hambledon that you realise how far you have climbed. There is only one steep hill and that is when you leave Hambledon.
Safety and Comfort: No problems.
Maps: Ordnance Survey Landranger 1: 50 000 Series - Sheets 185 and 196.
Map reference of start and finish - SU 613023.
Local Cycle Hire: Peter Hansford, 4 London Road, Horndean, Hants (Tel: 023 92592270), or Owens Cycles, Lavant Street, Petersfield (Tel: 01730 260446).
Other Refreshments on the Ride: The Horse and Jockey at Hipley and the Chairmakers are just over 1 mile (1.6km) from the start of the ride. On the outskirts of Denmead, at just over 2 miles (3.2km) there is the Fox and Hounds and the famous Bat and Ball pub is at 7 miles (11.2km). In Hambledon village there are a number of pubs and also Lotts Tea Room.
Travel by Car: The Travellers Rest is at Newtown which is just south of Soberton Heath. It is probably best approached from the south by using the B2177 and turning north at North Boarhunt.

Background ....

The best part of this ride takes us through some really pleasant country lanes, that are ideal for cycling. Inevitably you are likely to encounter some light traffic on the wider lanes and the occasional 'B' road which you have to cross or follow for a short stretch, but the route adheres in the main to the quieter country lanes. It is not difficult cycling but you will have to tackle the occasional gradient. It is all too easy to sometimes forget that reasonably steep climbs are rewarded with excellent downhill runs. A great way to cool down after your physical exertions.

Although this cycle ride begins at The Traveller's Rest in Newtown, there are many other pubs along the route that you may wish to visit. There is for example the Horse and Jockey situated just before Junction C, on the sketch map. The sign outside the Horse and Jockey commemorates a locally trained horse known as The Lamb who won the Grand National twice - in 1868 and 1871.

Places to explore around the route ....

Braodhalfpenny Down: The name of the Hambledon Cricket Ground at Broadhalfpenny Down is well known to cricket-lovers almost everywhere, and although it is often said to be the birthplace of cricket, it is probably more accurate to describe it as the nursery. The Hambledon Club was founded by a group of wealthy enthusiasts around 1750 and it had a brief period of cricketing glory that ended at the close of the 18th century. During this time the club beat All-England, Kent and Surrey teams, and over a ten year period beat England twenty nine times, the biggest margin being an innings and 168 runs. The reason that the exploits of the Hambledon club are so notable is undoubtedly due to the Nyren family. Richard Nyren was taught to play cricket by his uncle, Richard Newland (one of the truly great 18th century cricketers) in Slindon, Sussex. Richard Nyren later set up as landlord of the Hambledon public house known as the Hutt, which became the present Bat and Ball (see below). By 1771 Nyren had taken over a further public house in the village - The George - and he was well placed to provide the entertainment and refreshments for the matches. While Richard played a role of "general" to the team, his son John was also one of the earliest of a long line of Hampshire cricket writers, and this ensured that the deeds of the Hambledon club were recorded for us to read.

The Bat and Ball: The pub is grandly placed on Broadhalfpenny Down. It is 17th century and is situated next to the famous ground at Broadhalfpenny Down. There is a stone memorial opposite the inn that commemorates some of the famous years of the Hambledon Cricket Club from 1750-1787. A few years ago, the company that owned the Bat and Ball re-named it "Natterjacks". We could not imagine a more inappropriate name for a pub on top of a dry chalk down. Thankfully it has now been given back its rightful title.

Cycle Ride Directions ....

A. 0.0 (0.0): From the Travellers Rest car park, turn right onto the road.

B. 0.7 (0.7): At the junction, turn left into what is quite a fast, busy road.

C. 0.7 (1.4): This junction is by the Chairmakers pub, turn right following the signpost to Denmead, Waterlooville and Catherington.

D. 0.6 (2.0): Turn left up towards the Fox and Hounds, (the road was unmarked at the time of riding).

E. 0.5 (2.5): When you reach the junction by the Fox and Hounds, continue along the road opposite.

F. 0.2 (2.7): At the end of Upper Crabbick Lane, turn right.

G. 0.3 (3.0): Turn left onto the B2150 signposted Droxford 5¼ and Hambledon 1½.

H. 0.1 (3.1): Turn right off the B2150. Take great care when doing this as the road is very fast.

I. 0.2 (3.3): Just past Rookwood Cottage, take the turning on the right which is signposted "Lovedean 3, Catherington 3¾".

J. 0.4 (3.7): At the staggered crossroads, continue straight on.

K. 0.3 (4.0): Do not go down White Horse Lane, but continue on the same route under the power lines.

L. 0.2 (4.2): Turn left at the staggered cross roads - you will again pass under the high voltage power lines.

M. 0.9 (5.1): Pass the wood, brick and flint buildings on your left and ignore the turning off to the right. Pass the boarding kennels and enjoy the downhill run which is to follow.

N. 1.6 (6.7): You come to the end of Old Mill Lane where you will see the Bat and Ball Inn opposite. Turn left at this junction which is signposted

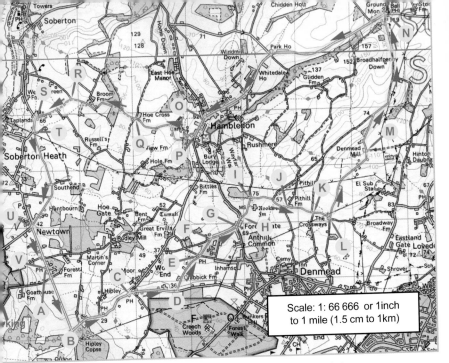

Hambledon and Fareham. (Be careful as this is a blind junction).

O. 2.3 (9.0): When you reach the junction in Hambledon, turn left into Green Lane which is signposted Waterlooville and Denmead.

P. 0.2 (9.2): Turn right off the main road by Lotts General Store and Tea-room. You then climb quite a steep hill (14% gradient).

Q. 0.9 (10.1): Carry straight on at the crossroads. Your route is signposted to Swanmore and Bishops Waltham.

R. 0.9 (11.0): Swing left as signposted "Soberton Heath 1¼, Newtown 1¾".

S. 0.4 (11.4): At Taplands, turn left, signposted "Newtown 1¼, Southwick 2"and you will pass Half Acre Cottage on the left.

T. 0.1(11.5): Bear left off the road into Ingoldfield Lane.

U. 1.1 (12.6): Turn left onto Church Road signposted "Southwick 3, Portsmouth 10" and continue along this until you arrive back at the Travellers Rest.

V. 0.4 (13.0): Arrive back at the Travellers Rest.

Pub File..........

The Travellers Rest: Cyclists are welcome and you can get your book 'pubberstamped' here. Opening times are 11.30am to 3.30pm and 6pm to 11pm on Mondays to Saturdays; midday to 3.30pm and 7pm to 10.30pm on Sundays. There is a non-smoking dining area, an extensive range of bar food, including 'superb' home-made pies and a daily 'Specials' board. Food is available daily from midday to 2pm and 7pm to 9.30pm every day, except Sunday evenings in winter. The pub serves three different real ales. Children are allowed into at least one area of the pub. Dogs are permitted if kept on a lead. The licensee is happy for cyclists to park their cars in the car park providing they patronise the pub before or after their ride. (Tel: 01329 833263).

SOUTHWICK AND THE OLD FOREST OF BERE

(Where we explore the clay vale behind Portsdown Hill)

Fact File..........

Starting Point: This ride starts from the Red Lion at Southwick.

Alternative Parking and Start Point: If you do not wish to park at the Red Lion then utilise the D-Day Memorial Village Hall Car Park. This is free and can be found at the south end of the village by taking the turning for HMS Dryad and then turning left by the retired sailors' cottages.

Distance: Allow 2 hours for this ride, the distance is 11.7 miles (18.8km).

Classification: 'Moderate' - this an easy ride that is undulating in places.

Surface and Nature of Route: The whole of this ride takes place on unclassified country roads that are delightfully quiet.

Safety and Comfort: No problems.

Maps: Ordnance Survey Landranger 1: 50 000 Series - Sheet 196.

Map reference of start and finish - SU 627087.

Local Cycle Hire: Peter Hansford, 4 London Road, Horndean, Hants (Tel: 023 92592270), or Owens Cycles, Lavant Street, Petersfield (Tel: 01730 260446).

Other Refreshments on the Ride: The Travellers Rest in Newtown at 3 miles (4.8km). The Horse and Jockey at Hipley and the Chairmakers Arms, both at approximately 8 miles (12.9km). There is also the other "Lion" in Southwick - the Golden Lion.

Travel by Car: Southwick lies immediately to the north of the B2177 Havant to Wickham road. The Red Lion is situated close to the church near the centre of the village, in the High Street.

Background ....

This ride commences from the Red Lion in the attractive village of Southwick. It heads due north climbing a slight incline via Newtown to Soberton Heath before turning to head south on the downhill run, hopefully with the sun in your face all the

way. The route uses the quietest of lanes, except perhaps for the section

The village school - Southwick

Thatched cottages - Southwick

between Points D and E where the road, although not generally busy, can be fast due to its straightness. Altogether this is a short easy ride around the lanes of Hampshire that you should find relaxing and enjoyable.

Cycle Ride Directions ....

A. 0.0 (0.0): From the Red Lion Car Park, turn right and then left by the thatched cottages into Back Lane.

B. 0.3 (0.3): At the end of Back Lane, turn right onto a wider road to cross the small river. Immediately after crossing the river, turn right again into Common Lane.

C. 1.3 (1.6): At the point where Common Lane ends at a T-junction marked with chevrons on a wider road, bear right.

D. 0.4 (2.0): Leave the road at a point where it swings sharp right, by turning left (effectively keeping straight on), as signposted "Newtown and Soberton".

Places to explore around the route ....

Southwick: There are several Southwicks in England, but I believe that this is the only one pronounced "Suthick". It sits on rising ground between two branches of the River Wallington and nestles in the shadow of Portsdown Hill. It is a pretty little village of old cottages, some thatched, some of herring-bone brick and some of board that provide a beautiful variety of styles. However, this variety is counterbalanced by the uniformity of its colour scheme - the Southwick Estate which seems to control the majority of the village decrees that the doors shall be maroon and the window frames cream. In the summer months, Southwick is one of those villages where you will always find flowers and vegetables for sale at the roadside at prices that you would be foolish to resist.

Forest of Bere: After leaving Southwick, you will be passing through heavy clay land that was once part of the Forest of Bere. Although only odd fragments now remain of the forested land, it does have a "feel" all of its own, with its undulating fields and the high-pitched roofs of the farm houses. At one time the forest was around 8 miles (12.9km) wide and stretched from Denmead and Rowlands Castle in the east to Kings Somborne and the River Test in the west. The largest fragment that now remains is West Walk and a short detour from Newtown (by turning left at Point E) will take you there. Another remaining fragment is Creech Walk - which lies alongside the route near Point L.

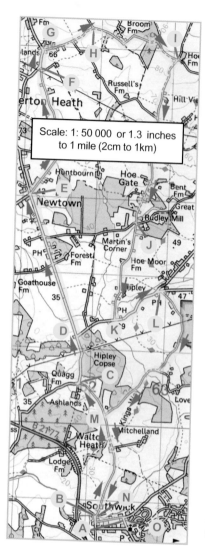

E. 1.3 (3.3): In Newtown, turn right as signposted to "Southend and Ingoldfield".

F. 1.1 (4.4): Bear right at the give-way junction "Soberton 1¼, Droxford 2½".

G. 0.2 (4.6): Turn right as signposted to "Hoe Cross 1½, Hambledon 2½".

H. 0.6 (5.2): Turn right as signposted to "Hambledon 2, Denmead 3½".

I. 0.9 (6.1): Turn right as signposted to "Southwick 4½, Fareham 7¼".

J. 1.4 (7.5): At Rudley Mill, turn left at the T Junction, to cross the small bridge with white railings and then immediately turn right, signposted "Southwick 3, Fareham 5¾".

K. 0.9 (8.4): At the end of Bunns Lane, you will come to a T-Junction, turn left to pass the Horse and Jockey.

L. 0.5 (8.9): By the Chairmakers Arms, turn right into Forest Lane to "Denmead 1¼, Waterlooville 4¼, Catherington 5¼" and immediately right again into Apless Lane.

M. 1.4 (10.3): At the end of Beckford Lane, turn left to rejoin your outgoing route.

N. 0.9 (11.2): Common Lane ends, and you turn left over the small bridge and immediately turn left into Back Lane. At the end of Back Lane, turn right into the High Street.

O. 0.5 (11.7): Arrive back at the Red Lion.

Pub File..........

The Red Lion: Cyclists are welcome and you can get your book 'pubberstamped' here. Opening times are 11am to 3pm and 6pm to 11pm on Tuesdays to Saturdays; midday to 3pm and 6pm to 10.30pm on Sundays. There is a restaurant, an extensive range of bar food and a daily 'Specials' board. Food is available from midday to 2pm and 6pm to 9.30pm on Tuesdays to Saturdays; midday to 2pm and 6pm to 9pm on Sundays, but it is advisable to book a table if you want to eat. The pub serves real ale. Children are welcome and are allowed into at least one area of the premises. Dogs are not permitted into the pub. The licensee is happy for cyclists to park their cars in the car park providing they patronise the pub before or after their ride. (Tel: 023 92377223).

THE HAYLING BILLY LEISURE TRAIL

(Where we explore the old railway line on Hayling Island)

Fact File..........

Starting Point: This ride starts from the public car park close to the Ship Inn at Langstone.

Alternative Parking and Start Point: It is also possible to park at one of the beach car parks.

Distance: Allow 2 hours for this ride, the distance is 9.3 miles (15km).

Surface and Nature of Route: The first half of the ride is on the cycle trail. This is often 6.5 yards (6 metres) wide and the surface is usually good, either being of a fine shingle or scalpings. Horses are usually separated from cyclists and pedestrians and this means that the surface tends to be well preserved.

Classification: 'Gentle' - an extremely flat ride with not a hill to be seen!

Safety and Comfort: Take care between Points E and G as this is one of the main routes onto the island and is consequently busy.

Maps: Ordnance Survey Landranger 1: 50 000 Series - Sheet 197.

Map reference of start and finish - SU 717050.

Local Cycle Hire: Barreg Cycles, Main Road, Fishbourne, Chichester, West Sussex, PO18 8AN (Tel: 01243 786104).

Other Refreshments on the Ride: Also close to Langstone Car Park at the start of the route, is the Royal Oak. The Maypole Inn and Yew Tree can be found at around 7 miles (11.2km).

Travel by Car: Langstone is immediately south of Havant and separated from it by the A27(T). Take the exit from the A27(T) signed A3023 Hayling.

Travel by Rail: Havant Railway Station is only 2 miles (3.2km) away. You can use the Hayling Billy Trail for a good part of this distance (from Havant Museum to Langstone Bridge).

Background ....

Hayling Island is not readily associated with the peace and tranquillity of a relaxing Sunday afternoon cycle ride. The image that more readily springs to mind is of traffic creeping nose to tail across Langstone Bridge, and all the way to the beach on an August Bank Holiday.

But, waiting to be discovered on the west side of the island is a green "lung" that enables you to ride or walk away from the motor car and suburbia for a while, and to enjoy a surprisingly rich flora and fauna. This is the Hayling Billy Leisure Trail - and it forms the first part of this circular ride. The trail is owned and maintained by Hampshire County Council, is completely traffic-free and takes you to the south of the island in complete safety. The second part of the ride between Points E and H is fairly heavy with traffic, while the final part of the ride is charming and fairly rural and takes you through the pleasant settlements of Tye and North Hayling. However, if you are cycling with young children, due to the busy nature of the middle part of the ride, we would strongly advise you to restrict your route to a "there and back" ride along the cycle trail. This will provide you with nearly 6 miles (9.6km) of wonderful traffic-free cycling.

Places to explore around the route ....

The Hayling Billy Railway: The line was opened in 1867 and played a large part in transporting the many city dwellers to the resort of South Hayling. It also had a role in transporting produce to and from the island. The branch line began at Havant Station and continued south under the Havant to Emsworth road, past the old Havant Town Hall, across the Havant to Hayling road via a level crossing to Langstone Station. The bridge then took the line across Langstone Harbour and was 1100 feet (335 metres) long, made of wood with concrete piles and had a central opening span to permit the passing of ships. The bridge was lightly constructed and was only capable of carrying a light engine - a factor that was to limit the use of the railway throughout its life. The railway was closed as part of the Beeching railway cuts in 1963.

Hayling Village: The island is divided by a natural waist into two parts - North and South Hayling. North Hayling is now connected to Langstone by a bridge, but prior to 1824, when a tollbridge was built, the only method of accessing Hayling was to use the Wadeway (in effect a ford) across the channel at low tide. A visit to the beautiful and ancient St Peter's Church that we pass on the ride is a very pleasant experience. It was built around 1140 by the monks of Jumiéges and was originally known as Northwode chapel. Some of the stone used in the nave is believed to have been prepared in Normandy before being shipped to Hayling. Of interest outside the church is the 800-year-old yew tree. An interesting grave can be found in the churchyard near the car park - it is the resting place of Princess Yourievsky, who was a member of the ill-fated royal Russian family who lived in North Hayling for many years. A well-presented and informative guide is available inside the church.

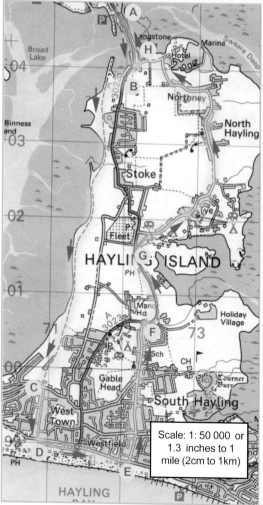

Scale: 1: 50 000 or 1.3 inches to 1 mile (2cm to 1km)

Langstone - looking toward the Royal Oak and Langstone Mill

Cycle Ride Directions ....

A. 0.0 (0.0): From the Langstone Car Park, cycle over the bridge and continue until you see the blue "Hayling Billy" sign.

B. 0.6 (0.6): Carefully cross the road and follow the directions to the cycle trail. Start cycling the trail.

C. 2.9 (3.5): Leave the trail at the site of the old Hayling Island Station at the southern end of the line, and cross Sinah Lane to continue in a similar direction along Staunton Avenue.

D. 0.4 (3.9): At the end of Staunton Avenue, turn left onto the Sea Front, and cross the roundabout by the Funland beach amusements.

E. 0.9 (4.8): Turn left into Seagrove Avenue signposted "Mengham and Havant (A3023)".

F. 1.1 (5.9): At the end of Church Road, turn right by the roundabout onto Havant Road (A3023). Take care here, this is a busy road and it may be best to cross the roundabout on foot using the traffic islands.

G. 0.8 (6.7): Turn right into Yew Tree Road and after about 300 yards (274 metres), turn right at the give way junction and continue to follow this road through North Hayling.

H. 2.6 (9.3): You will meet the A3023 again close to Langstone Bridge, turn right here and cycle back over the bridge to the car park by the Ship.

Pub File..........

The Ship Inn: Cyclists are welcome and you can get your book 'pubberstamped' here. Opening times are 11am to 11pm on Mondays to Saturdays and midday to 10.30pm on Sundays. There is a family dining area upstairs, an extensive range of bar food and a daily 'Specials' board. Food is available daily from midday to 2pm and 6.30pm to 9.30pm, but on Sunday it is available all day, from midday through to 9pm. The pub serves real ale. Children are welcome and are allowed into at least one area of the premises. Dogs are permitted downstairs if kept on a lead. Langstone Car Park (free) surrounds the pub. (Tel: 023 92471719).

EDWARD THOMAS COUNTRY

(Where we visit a pub with no name and a village that is lucky to have its church)

Fact File.........

Starting Point: This walk starts at the White Horse Inn (known by most as the "pub with no name"), at Priors Dean near Petersfield.

Alternative Parking and Start Point: This ride follows narrow country lanes and small hamlets and we were unable to find any alternative to parking at the White Horse.

Distance: Allow 1 hour 40 minutes for this ride. The distance is 9.5 miles (15.3km).

Classification: 'Gentle' - no significant hills.

Surface and Nature of Route: This ride takes place on very quiet country lanes.

Safety and Comfort: No problems.

Maps: Ordnance Survey Landranger 1: 50 000 Series - Sheet 186.

Map reference of start and finish - SU 714290.

Local Cycle Hire: Owens Cycles, Lavant Street, Petersfield (Tel: 01730 260446).

Other Refreshments on the Ride: None.

Travel by Car: Assuming you travel by the A3, take the main Petersfield exit and drive into Petersfield for about 0.5 mile (0.8km) and then turn left at the roundabout and head north towards Steep and then on towards the high downs. About 2 miles (3.2km) after the Trooper Public House you will see the pub signpost with the sign missing. Turn right here and turn right again into the second track near a smaller but similar pub sign.

Background ....

This is a very peaceful ride that utilises the quiet, shady, and isolated lanes, on the high plateau to the north of Petersfield. One of the disadvantages of riding such quiet lanes is the poor state of signposting. Our observations on the standard of Hampshire signposting have been made before, but it is on these lanes that the things probably reach their lowest point. Put simply, there are effectively no signposts. Of the very few that we did see, the paint had peeled off to reveal earlier markings relating to a previous use in another part of the county, and so they were completely useless. So, you will need to follow the directions and map very carefully.

Towards the end of the ride, after leaving Froxfield Green, you will experience fine views of the vale below and the South Downs in the distance.

Cycle Ride Directions ....

A. 0.0 (0.0): From the pub car park, follow the gravel track back out to the lane, and turn right down the hill.

B. 0.6 (0.6): Bear left off the lane by the grass triangle, there were no signs at the time of writing.

Places to explore around the route ....

The White Horse Inn: We have already mentioned in Walk 11 that the high Downland area north of Petersfield is very much the countryside of Edward Thomas the writer and poet. He lived there from 1906 until shortly before he died in France in the First World War in 1917. There are very few features of the area that have escaped the attention of his prose or poetry, and arguably one of his best known poems was written specifically about the White Horse Inn. It took him a long time to take the step to poetry and it appears that once that step was made, he became a more contented man. The first (and incidentally the longest) poem that he ever wrote was called "Up in the Wind" and was about this very pub:

.... Two roads cross, and not a house in sight
Except the 'White Horse' in this clump of beeches.

A question often asked is why is the pub in such an odd location, apparently in the middle of fields? The answer seems to be that before the common was enclosed and farmed, the old road from Petersfield to Alton came across the plateau past the inn. This was an important road to Oxford and the Midlands and there was a need for refreshment and repairs. In fact, the room that is now the lower bar was at one time the smithy associated with the pub. This road is now long gone and we are left with this delightful old pub in the middle of nowhere.

Froxfield Green: This is a very pleasant spot with the old farmhouse, war memorial and church surrounding the green. There has been a church at Froxfield Green since the early 12th century. However, information inside the church will tell you that the church is not as old as it looks, and there was an earlier one that was removed, only to be built again. A consistory court agreed to the construction of a larger parish church at nearby High Cross and the old church by the green was demolished the day after the last service on 3rd March 1861. The new church incorporated some of the Norman arches of the old church. Fortunately, William Nicholson, whose fortune was made from gin, we believe, and who lived at nearby Basing Park, decided that the decision to remove the church was wrong and granted £1250 to enable the construction of the present church on the original site of the ancient building.

C. 0.9 (1.5): Turn left at the main road. This is a fast road, so take great care whilst cycling along it for the short distance.

D. 0.3 (1.8): Turn right off the main road into Alexanders Lane, signposted "Alexander, Hurst".

E. 1.1 (2.9): At the end of Alexanders Lane, by a lovely old thatched cottage and a post box - go straight on into Hurst Lane.

F. 0.3 (3.2): At the "no through

Evening at the White Horse Inn

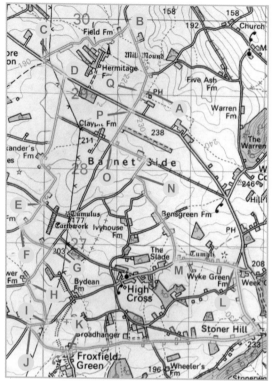

J. 0.2 (4.5): At the cross-roads, turn left and pass under the power lines.

K. 0.4 (4.9): At Froxfield Green, by the lovely old church and war memorial, turn left as signposted to "Stoner Hill and High Cross". Ignore all turnings off this road until you arrive at the give-way and cross roads.

L. 2.2 (7.1): Turn left here - this is signposted to "Froxfield 1 and Privett 4".

M. 0.5 (7.6): Take the road immediately after Spencer's Barn, as directed to Blackmore and Bensgreen Farms.

N. 0.9 (8.5): Turn right at the T-Junction.

O. 0.4 (8.9): Turn right at the cross-roads opposite Claypits Lane.

P. 0.4 (9.3): Opposite the empty pub sign, cross over the main road into the lane opposite.

Q. 0.2 (9.5): You will see a smaller empty pub sign, turn right here to return to the White Horse.

road" sign, turn left.

G. 0.3 (3.5): At the junction, turn right, and pass under the electric wires (no signpost here).

H. 0.4 (3.9): Just after you pass Bower Farm, bear left.

I. 0.4 (4.3): This junction is next to a large electricity pylon. Turn right as directed to "Froxfield Green and East Meon".

Pub File.........

The White Horse Inn: Cyclists are welcome and you can get your book 'pubberstamped' here. Opening times are 11am to 2.30pm and 6pm to 11pm on Mondays to Saturdays; midday to 3pm and 7pm to 10.30pm on Sundays. There is a restaurant, an extensive range of bar food and a daily 'Specials' board. Food is available daily during opening hours. The pub serves real ale. Children are allowed into at least one area of the pub. Dogs are permitted if kept on a lead. Camping and Caravans are welcome. The licensee is happy for cyclists to park their cars in the car park providing they patronise the pub before or after their ride. (Tel: 01420 588387).

THE GLORY OF THE SOUTH DOWNS

(Along the ridge of the downs to return via some of the best pubs in the South Country)

Fact File..........

Starting Point: This ride starts from the Master Robert pub in Buriton.

Alternative Parking and Start Point: There is a free car park at Halls Hill. This is on the right-hand side of Kiln Lane where it intersects with the South Downs Way, at Point B on the map.

Distance: Allow 3 hours for this ride, the distance is 17.1 miles (27.5km).

Surface and Nature of Route: The early part of the ride follows the South Downs Way over a combination of surfaced byways and unsurfaced bridleways. On this section you will be unlucky if you meet any traffic at all. The remainder of the ride follows the quiet country lanes that are a feature of the Rother Valley.

Classification: 'Could make you puff' - the ride starts off with a very steep climb up Kiln Lane and the following 4 miles (6.4km) are on a fairly undulating part of the South Downs Way.

Safety and Comfort: A section of this ride is off-road and therefore it is especially important to wear a helmet when going downhill at speed.

Maps: Ordnance Survey Landranger 1: 50 000 Series - Sheet 197.

Map reference of start and finish - SU 737202.

Local Cycle Hire: Local Cycle Hire: Owens Cycles, Lavant Street, Petersfield (Tel: 01730 260446). Peter Hansford, 4 London Road, Horndean, Hants (Tel: 023 92592270).

Other Refreshments on the Ride: Once you have left the ridge and you are at the foot of the downs, you will find that the area abounds with some of the best pubs that can be found in the South Country. Apart from the Master Robert, alongside the route there are (in order): the Three Horseshoes in Elsted at 6 miles (9.7km), the Elsted Inn at 8 miles (12.9km), and the Five Bells in Buriton at 16 miles (25.7km). In addition, close to the route there is the White Hart and the Ship in South Harting.

Travel by Car: Travel via the A3 and about 2 miles (3.2km) south of Petersfield you will see the turning for Buriton.

Background ....

Over the years, we have gained much family enjoyment out of our expeditions along the South Downs Way that runs from Buriton, via Chanctonbury Ring and Ditchling Beacon to Beachy Head. We have walked it over the course of a week, cycled it over 3 days, and enjoyed countless 1-day walks in all seasons. Its principle attraction lies in the fact that when you are on these smooth whale-backed downs you have a feeling of remoteness, peace and tranquility, and yet you are never more than a few miles away from food or accommodation.

Cycle Ride Directions ....

A. 0.0 (0.0): From the Master Robert, cycle up Kiln Lane, signposted "Chalton 4, Finchdean 6".

B. 0.4 (0.4): At the top of the hill, by Halls Hill Car Park, take the South Downs Way by following the route marked Dean Barn. After about 0.3 miles (0.5km) the surfacing ends and the South Downs Way becomes a track, until the Coulters Dean Nature Reserve, when it becomes surfaced again.

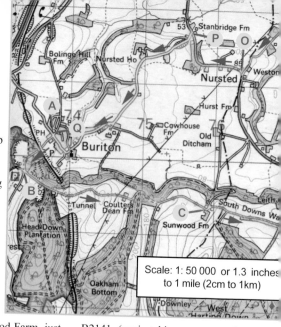

C. 1.8 (2.2): At Sunwood Farm, just after the surfaced road turns sharply, turn right off the road to continue to follow the South Downs Way.

D. 1.6 (3.8): When you meet the B2146, cross straight over it (taking great care as the visibility is bad) to take the track opposite and continue to follow the South Downs Way.

E. 0.5 (4.3): When you meet the B2141, (again taking great care due to poor visibility), turn left for about 30 yards (27km) and then turn right off the B2141 to take the quiet lane down a steep hill.

F. 0.9 (5.2): At the end of the lane, turn right and continue through Elsted to pass the village hall and the Three Horseshoes.

G. 2.8 (8.0): At the Elsted Inn junction, turn left as signposted "Trotton 2, Dunford 1".

H. 0.9 (8.9): At a give way junction, turn left as directed to "Nyewood 2",

Places to explore around the route ....

Buriton: You will notice as you pass through the villages of Buriton and Harting at the foot of the downs, that many of the old buildings are built of a very attractive white stone, often set off with corners of red brick. These villages are sometimes known as the "Clunch" Villages - clunch being the name of this local creamy-white building stone that has such a beautiful appearance. Buriton has some particularly fine examples, and one of these is the Five Bells pub. If you look carefully, the Five Bells has small black spots surrounding each stone, forming a pattern. These are called 'Penny Nails" and were of snob value in times past and an indication of prosperity.

South Harting: Although this ride does not pass directly through South Harting, a short detour will take you there. The village sits comfortably at the foot of the downs, with its pale green church spire standing out from the darker green of the downs towering above. The village once featured in a promotional film, designed to tempt North Americans to come to England - it is not difficult to understand why, as it is such a perfect example of a picturesque South Country village; combining the warmth of its creamy clunch walls with a perfect setting.

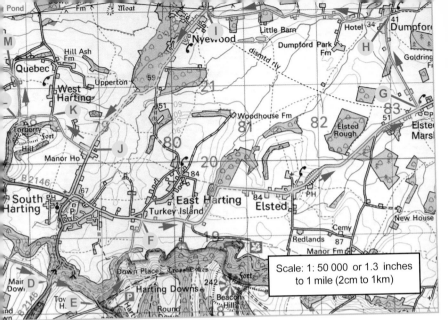

along a road marked as a "single track road with passing places".

I. 1.7 (10.6): At a further give-way junction, underneath the power lines, turn left into Nyewood.

J. 1.6 (12.2): Avoid South Harting (unless you need some refreshments at one of the pubs or the excellent village shop complete with delicatessen) by turning right toward West Harting.

K. 0.5 (12.7): By the timber-framed cottage and ex-pub known as the Old Greyhound, turn left as directed to "Petersfield 4".

L. 0.3 (13.0): Turn right at the junction, signposted to Rogate.

M. 0.3 (13.3): At the next small junction turn left for Goose Green.

N. 0.7 (14.0): Bear left at the little triangular junction in Goose Green.

O. 0.6 (14.6): Bear right at the main road and re-enter Hampshire.

P. 0.6 (15.2): Turn left as signposted to "Buriton 1½ miles". This is a long and meandering route that will eventually lead you back past the duck pond and through the village.

Q. 1.9 (17.1): Arrive back at the Master Robert.

Pub File..........

The Master Robert: Cyclists are welcome and you can get your book 'pubberstamped' here.Opening times are 11.45am to 3pm and 6pm to 11pm from Mondays to Saturdays and on Sundays from midday to 3pm and 7pm to 10.30pm. There is a restaurant, an extensive range of bar food and a daily 'Specials' board. Food times are midday to 2.30pm and 6.30pm to 9.30pm every day except on Sunday evenings. The pub serves real ale. Children are welcome and are allowed into at least one area of the premises. Dogs are permitted if kept on a lead. Some overnight accommodation is available. Cyclists are welcome to park their cars in the pub car park providing they patronise the pub before or after their ride. (Tel: 01730 267275).

THE PENINSULAR FLATLANDS OF CHICHESTER

(Where we learn a little about Bosham and visit Chidham again)

Fact File.........

Starting Point: This ride starts from the Berkeley Arms in Bosham.

Alternative Parking and Start Point: An alternative parking place at reasonable cost is Bosham Pay and Display Car Park.

Distance: Allow 2 hours 40 minutes for this ride, the distance is 15.8 miles (25.4km).

Classification: 'Gentle' - an exceptionally flat ride.

Surface and Nature of Route: For the most part this ride takes place on quiet country lanes. There is a short section of 1.1 miles (1.8km) on the A259, but there is a pavement where you may wheel your bikes if you wish.

Safety and Comfort: Take care when crossing the A259 as it is a fast road.

Maps: Ordnance Survey Landranger 1: 50 000 Series - Sheet 197.

Map reference of start and finish - SU 810043.

Local Cycle Hire: Cycles can be hired from Hargroves Cycles, 2 Christchurch Buildings, Chichester, West Sussex, PO19 1DP (Tel: 01243 537337), or Barreg Cycles, Main Road, Fishbourne, Chichester, West Sussex, PO18 8AN (Tel: 01243 786104).

Other Refreshments on the Ride: There are several opportunities in Bosham. There is the Millstream Hotel (known for its afternoon cream teas), and Mariners Coffee Shop. The Anchor Bleu is a characterful pub, often full of sailing folk. Around the route there is the John Barleycorn at 11 miles (17.7km), the Old House at Home at 12 miles (19.3km), the Bosham Inn at 14 miles (22.4km) and the White Swan at 15 miles (24.1km).

Travel by Car: Bosham lies just south of the old A27 Chichester to Havant Road (now the A259).

Travel by Rail: This ride can easily be started from either Bosham and Nutbourne Stations.

Background ....

This ride is almost completely flat and takes place on the quietest of country lanes. There are many places to stop for refreshment, making this a very easy and relaxing ride. However, you need to be aware of the tides for this ride as Shore Road floods at high tide.

If you start the ride from the Berkeley Arms, it would be sensible to have a look at Shore Road beforehand. Alternatively you could check the tide times before you start the ride. If Shore Road is flooded then use the map to find an alternative route. If you decide to park in Shore Road then you need to be even more careful. A few years ago, an old friend of ours was doing one of our walks from Bosham, and he unwisely decided to park his brand new company car there. He really enjoyed his walk taking about 4 hours altogether, including a leisurely lunch. On his

Bosham Harbour

---

return he found his life shattered, with his car almost completely underwater due to a particularly high tide. Sea water is not compatible with brand new engines, or anything to do with cars for that matter, and his (and the company's) pride and joy had to be completely written off.

Cycle Ride Directions ....

A. 0.0 (0.0): From the Berkeley Arms, turn right into Bosham Lane and cycle toward the harbour.

B. 0.5 (0.5): As you meet the foreshore, turn left into Shore Road to follow the water's edge.

C. 0.4 (0.9): At the junction with Stumps Lane, turn right to continue following Shore Road around the foreshore.

D. 0.7 (1.6): Leave Shore Road and the foreshore and join Lower Hone Lane. At Bosham Hoe the name of the road changes to Smugglers Lane.

E. 1.9 (3.5): Turn right as signposted to "Fishbourne and Chichester".

F. 2.1 (5.6): Where Old Park Lane meets the A259, turn right and then immediately left into Blackboy Lane (opposite the Blackboy Inn).

G. 1.3 (6.9): Leave Blackboy Lane by turning left into Clay Lane.

H. 1.7 (8.6): Turn left into Southbrook Road (signposted to "Woodmancote") to continue on the South Coast Cycle Route.

I. 0.5 (9.1): Turn left as directed to "Hambrook", remaining on the South Coast Cycle Route.

J. 0.9 (10.0): At a cross roads, turn left for "Hambrook and Nutbourne (A259)".

K. 1.1 (11.1): Leave Broad Road to cross the busy A259 (take care here) and then join Cot Lane which takes you down to Chidham village.

L. 1.4 (12.5): Swing right into Chidham Lane, signposted "Chidham East and Cobnor".

M. 1.6 (14.1): Turn right onto the

Places to explore around the route ....

Bosham village: For visitors to Bosham and those new to Sussex ways, there is a quirk of pronunciation to be mastered. Never rhyme the first syllable of Bosham with posh. The emphasis should be on the last syllable and pronounced "Bozham". There are many coastal settlements that lay claim to the site of King Canute's realisation of the limits of his royal power. But the inhabitants of Bosham have it, that this is the place where it really happened. He certainly lived here for a while and one of his daughters lies buried in the church. Bosham church is featured in the Bayeux Tapestry, where Harold can be seen entering to take the Sacrament.

Chidham: Chidham is a charming village lying on a flat windswept peninsula set between Thorney Island and Bosham. The church of St Mary's somehow fits in perfectly, being not too large and not too small. It is a simple church officially described as being of stone and of Early English style. It dates from 1220 (if one forgets the earlier church on the site) and was restored in 1864.

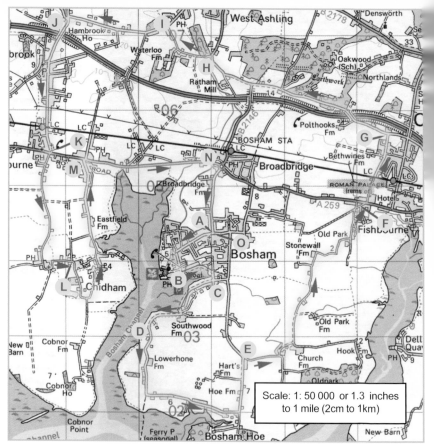

Scale: 1: 50 000 or 1.3 inches to 1 mile (2cm to 1km)

A259. Please note that this is a busy road. There is a pavement running alongside this road (often on both sides) so you may wish to use this.

N. 1.1 (15.2): At the Bosham roundabout, turn right as signposted to "Bosham Church and Quay".

O. 1.6 (15.8): Arrive back at the Berkeley Arms.

Pub File..........

The Berkeley Arms: Cyclists are welcome and you can get your book 'pubberstamped' here. Opening times vary according to the season. From June to August (inclusive) the pub is open from 11am to 11pm on Mondays to Saturdays; midday to 10.30pm on Sundays. From September to May the pub is open from 11am to 3pm and 6pm to 11.30pm Mondays to Fridays; 11am to 11.30pm on Saturdays and Sundays. There is a restaurant, an extensive range of bar food and a daily 'Specials' board. Food is available every day midday to 9pm during summer opening times and midday to 2.30pm and 6pm to 9pm at all other times of the year. The pub serves real ale. Children are welcome and are allowed into at least one area of the premises. Dogs are permitted if kept on a lead. The licensee is happy for cyclists to park their cars in the car park providing they patronise the pub before or after their ride. (Tel: 01243 573167).

A VISIT TO THE SHEPHERDS' CHURCH

(Where we cycle through some delightfully-named villages along the foot of the South Downs)

Fact File.........

Starting Point: This ride starts from The Country Inn near Bepton at Point A on the map.

Alternative Parking and Start Point: An ideal alternative starting point is from the car park at Stedham Common.

Distance: Allow 2 hours for this ride, the distance is 12 miles (19.3km).

Surface and Nature of Route: This ride takes place on very quiet and narrow country lanes.

Classification: 'Gentle' - This ride is generally flat as it meanders around the valley of the Rother at the foot of the South Downs.

Safety and Comfort: A 0.4 mile (0.6km) section of this ride is on the fast and busy A272. Fortunately, there is a track intended for pedestrians set back a few feet from the road that you can utilise as you wish.

Maps: Ordnance Survey Landranger 1: 50 000 Series - Sheet 197.

Map reference of start and finish - SU 871205.

Local Cycle Hire: Sensible Bike Company, 71 Station Road, Liss, Hants (Tel: 01730 894884) (www.sensiblebike.co.uk).

Other Refreshments on the Ride: There is the Elsted Inn at Lower Elsted at 5.5 miles (8.8km) and also a pub in Stedham at 2 miles (3.2 km).

Travel by Car: The Country Inn lies about 1 mile (1.6km) south west of Midhurst.

Background ....

This ride starts at the Country Inn at Bepton and meanders around the Rother Valley before it returns in an easterly direction in the shadow of the beautiful South Downs. Although most of the ride is within sight of this most attractive stretch of downs, you get the benefit of the view without the pain. This is because the Rother Valley is how you would expect a river valley to be: flat and ideal cycling country, with many delight-fully quiet and narrow country lanes. This is also one of those parts of the world where even the place-names seem picturesque. Trotton, Treyford, Didling and Dumpford - they have a character all of their own and seem to roll off the tongue and match the setting of these villages perfectly.

The St Christopher signpost at Treyford

Places to explore around the route ....

The Shepherds' Church: This little gem can be found after about 7 miles (11.2km), close to Point M on the ride. It is definitely worth the small deviation and if ever we are walking or cycling in these parts we usually stop and sit on the memorial bench and enjoy a snack under the centuries-old yew tree. The church is consecrated to St Andrew, but is has been known as the Shepherds' Church for as long as people can remember, and no doubt it was named as such due to its use by the many shepherds who tended their flocks on the nearby downs. The Laudian altar rails are also interesting. These date from around 1640 and are an example of the beautiful woodwork of the period. They are known as Laudian altar rails because they were introduced by an Archbishop of Canterbury known as William Laud. At that time, it was perfectly normal for shepherds or other owners of dogs to bring them into church. Of course, the dogs were not always church-trained, and the balusters were designed to be sufficiently close to prevent even puppies from getting through.

The Saint Christopher Signpost: In Treyford you will see at the side of the road a very attractive and colourful waymarker, of a type most unusual in England, and more commonly found in southern Germany. It was thought to have been designed by Graily Hewitt, a distinguished calligrapher who lived nearby at Brook Cottage. It shows St Christopher carrying the baby Jesus and points in the direction of Harting. The signpost disappeared in the 1950s when a subsequent owner of the cottage moved away, and it was found in a dilapidated state in Essex. It has now been restored and returned to Treyford.

Cycle Ride Directions ....

A. 0.0 (0.0): Starting with your back to the Country Inn, turn right to cycle away from the junction.

B. 0.8 (0.8): At the main road (A272) turn right. You may wish to use the track on the right hand side of the road, as this is a fast and busy road.

C. 0.4 (1.2): Turn left off the main road (A272), in the direction of Woolbeding, Redford and Liphook. Take great care when crossing this road.

D. 0.7 (1.9): At the junction by one of the Woolbeding Farms, bear left as directed to "Liphook, Lynch and St Cuthman's" (although at the time of riding the signpost was decrepit and not reliable). The road is marked as a single-track road with passing places.

E. 0.5 (2.4): Take the left turning, signposted "Stedham" - be careful as this is easy to miss.

F. 0.4 (2.8): Take the second turning right (to Iping), after the turning to St Cuthman's School).

G. 0.3 (3.1): Ignore the "no through road" to the right and continue downhill.

H. 0.3 (3.4): By Hammerwood House continue downhill to the left of the grass triangle junction and continue left at the next junction to Midhurst and Elsted, (the signpost was missing the last time that we checked this route).

I. 0.9 (4.3): Carefully cross the busy A272 and take the lane almost opposite signposted to "Elsted 3, Harting 5". Follow this straight road, and you will pass the Elsted Inn.

J. 1.1 (5.4): Turn left following the signpost to "Treyford 1".

K. 1.0 (6.4): Carry straight on down the hill, following the signpost to "Cocking 5, Didling 2".

L. 0.3 (6.7): In Treyford, at the junction with the unusual and beautiful St Christopher fingerpost, swing left and pass by the white

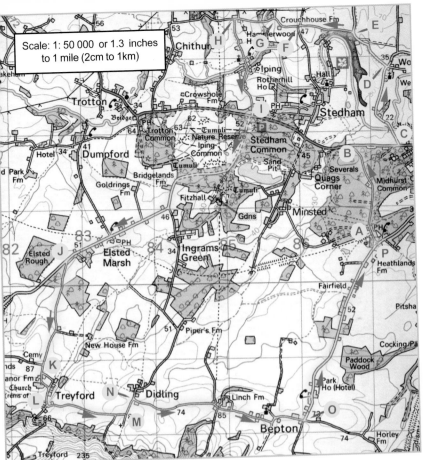

railings marking the stream, as directed "Didling 1, Cocking 4".

M. 0.7 (7.4): If you wish to visit the Shepherds' Church turn right at this point to follow the short lane. Otherwise turn left to continue on the ride.

N. 0.2 (7.6): Follow the road around to the right which takes you downhill.

This enables you to continue at the foot of the downs and is signposted "Bepton 2, Cocking 3".

O. 1.5 (9.1): By the white timber-framed cottage, turn left and follow the signpost that directs you to "Midhurst 3".

P. 1.8 (10.9): Turn left and you are back at the Country Inn.

Pub File..........

The Country Inn: Cyclists are welcome and you can get your book 'pubberstamped' here. Opening times are 11am to 4pm and 6pm to 11pm every day of the week. An extensive range of bar food is available and there is a 'Specials' board on Sundays. Food is available from midday to 2pm and 7pm to 9.30pm. The pub serves real ale. Children are welcome and are allowed into at least one area of the premises. Dogs are permitted if kept on a lead. The licensee is happy for cyclists to park their cars in the car park providing they patronise the pub before or after their ride. (Tel: 01730 813466).

THE CENTURION WAY

(Where we ride traffic-free around Chichester and enjoy cycling the flat country of the coastal plain)

Fact File..........

Starting Point: This ride starts from the Royal Oak at East Lavant.

Alternative Parking and Start Point: It is also possible to park in Mid Lavant by the river, and at the public car park at West Stoke (shown on the map).

Distance: Allow 2 hours for this ride, the distance is 12 miles (19.3km).

Surface and Nature of the Route: The Centurion Way is traffic-free, and has an excellent wide and smooth tarmac surface. The remainder of the ride is on quiet country roads.

Classification: 'Gentle' - an almost completely hill-free ride on the coastal plain around Chichester.

Safety and Comfort: Take great care when crossing the A286 in Mid Lavant as it is a busy road and visibility is very poor. Also take care when using the railway level crossings. Only cross the line when the green light shows and cross quickly.

Maps: Ordnance Survey Landranger 1: 50 000 Series - Sheet 197.

Map reference of start and finish - SU 863084.

Local Cycle Hire: Hargroves Cycles, 2 Christchurch Buildings, Chichester, West Sussex, PO19 1DP (Tel: 01243 537337), or Barreg Cycles, Main Road, Chichester, Fishbourne, West Sussex, PO18 8AN (Tel: 01243 786104).

Other Refreshments on the Ride: Close to the route are the Hunters Inn and the Earl of March, both in Mid Lavant. On the route itself at a distance of about 7 miles (11.2km) is the Richmond Arms at West Ashling, and at Funtington there is the Fox and Hounds at 8 miles (12.9km).

Travel by Car: East Lavant lies due north of Chichester. Turn off the A286 at Mid Lavant as directed to East Lavant.

Travel by Rail: Travel by rail to this ride is perfectly feasible, as there are three stations within 1 mile (1.6km) of the ride at Chichester, Fishbourne and Bosham.

Background ....

This ride is very flat and is a real gem. Starting off in East Lavant, it uses the excellent traffic-free Centurion Way to travel to the south of Chichester. It then picks up quiet lanes that form the South Coast Cycle Route to travel west to Funtington, before meandering along the foot of the downs on a quiet country lane through West Stoke.

The Centurion Way was built on the course of the Chichester to Midhurst Railway that was originally constructed in 1881 to improve access to London. There were 3 tunnels and 8 stations on the line, the most famous station being Goodwood due to the royal personages that alighted here during the Goodwood Race Meetings. The decline of the route started with the closure of passenger services in 1935 and in 1957 the section of the railway north of Lavant was completely closed.

Fishbourne Roman Palace: The site of these remains is about 1 mile (1.6km) from the route. The palace is one of the most extensive Roman sites in Britain. During the Roman invasion of AD43, Fishbourne was used as a military supply base. Later, civilians built their homes here and the palace was constructed in about AD75, possibly for a Celtic king, Tiberius Claudius Togidubnus. It was built on such a scale that it rivalled the imperial palaces of Rome itself. The remains of the palace were only discovered by workmen putting in a new water main in 1960.

West Stoke: You will, we are sure, be tempted to stop and look at the lovely church at West Stoke that the Saxons knew. It is a charming old church with its white walls, and the pyramid cap of its little tower that is over 800 years old. There are Roman tiles in the walls and inside there is a Saxon vestry door and an ancient painted mural that has recently been discovered and restored. Nearby, and about 1 mile (1.6km) to the north is Bow Hill and Kingley Vale.

Cycle Ride Directions ....

A. 0.0 (0.0): Assuming you have your back to the pub, turn right and cycle along the lane to Mid Lavant.  Immediately after crossing the bridge over the River Lavant, turn right to cycle along Sheepwash Lane, parallel with the river. The road becomes one-way for a short distance, but you are permitted to cycle on the pavement.

B. 0.4 (0.4): You meet the A286. Look for the sign on the opposite side of road marked "Public footpath access to Centurion Way". Cross this road very carefully as it is busy and visibility is poor at this point. Wheel your cycles along this short footpath and over the old railway bridge, turn left and pass through the barrier to descend to the Centurion Way.

C. 2.6 (3.0): When you are close to Bishop Luffa School, pass under the sculpture and after negotiating the metal barriers, swing right to follow the school boundary. At the end of the cycle path there is a bus turning area, turn right here (signposted to Roman Palace 3¾, Fishbourne 1, Bosham 3 and South Coast Cycle Route). Carefully cross the railway line using the level crossing and turn right at the road to continue on the South Coast Cycle Route.

D. 0.4 (3.4): Avoid passing under the A27 by turning right into Clay Lane and then crossing the railway line using the level crossing.

E. 0.8 (4.2): At the junction with Salthill Road, continue on Clay Lane and the South Coast Cycle Route following the sign for "W Ashling".

F. 1.9 (6.1): Turn left into Southbrook Road (signposted to Woodmancote) to continue on the South Coast Cycle Route.

G. 0.5 (6.6): Turn right as directed

The lovely church at West Stoke

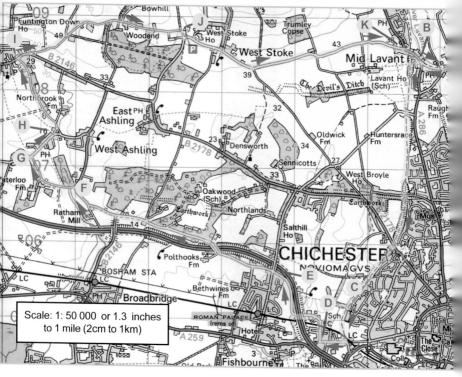

Scale: 1: 50 000 or 1.3 inches to 1 mile (2cm to 1km)

to "W and E Ashling and Chichester" leaving the South Coast Cycle Route at this point.

H. 0.3 (6.9): Almost immediately after passing the Richmond Arms pub, turn left into Watery Lane. A few yards later bear left at the give-way junction to cross the small bridge over the stream.

I. 0.8 (7.7): In Funtington, and at the end of Watery Lane you meet the B2146, turn right here and after a few yards leave the B2146 by turning left into a single track road (Downs Road).

J. 1.6 (9.3): Bear left at the give-way junction as signposted "West Stoke, Lavant".

K 2.0 (11.3): You will meet the A286 again by St Nicholas Church. Turn right here (we would strongly advise wheeling your cycles on the pavement for the short length of this road, you will have to switch sides of the road to ensure that you stay on the pavement). Turn left into Sheepwash Lane to re-trace your outgoing route.

L. 0.7 (12.0): Arrive back at the Royal Oak.

Pub File..........

The Royal Oak: Cyclists are welcome and you can get your book 'pubberstamped' here. Opening times are midday to 2.30pm and 6pm to 11pm every day except Sunday when the pub is open until 3pm. Food is available throughout opening hours. There is a restaurant and a daily 'Specials Board.' The pub does not sell snacks such as sandwiches, but instead provides light meals typically fish cakes, risotto and salads. The Royal Oak serves real ale. Children are welcome and are allowed into at least one area of the premises. Dogs are not permitted. Please do not park in the pub car park if you intend to go cycling as it is very small. Please park tidily in the village instead. (Tel: 01243 527434).

USEFUL INFORMATION

SAFETY, CLOTHING AND EQUIPMENT

THE WALKS

■ Summer

During the summer months, what you wear really depends on whether you like to "look the part". From April until October you can get by with the minimum of special clothes. The main aim is to be warm and dry, so the clothing that you take will depend very much on the weather forecast. As for footwear, whatever you wear should be comfortable and low-heeled. A lot has been said about the importance of having walking boots, but trainers or outdoor shoes are perfectly satisfactory. Also, remember to take a high factor sunscreen, a hat and a drink. Children should apply sunblock before setting off.

■ Winter

In the winter months, greater care should be taken not only from a safety point of view, but also to ensure enjoyment. The Downs upon which many of these walks take place are not high, but as they are close to the sea the weather can change very quickly. Again, the aim is to keep warm and dry. The exact clothing that you take depends on the weather on the day, but our advice is always to take more than you need. A large amount of body heat is lost from the head so it is a good idea to wear a hat. As far as footwear is concerned, it must be waterproof. Walking boots or stout walking shoes are preferable, but Wellington boots, although not ideal, should be adequate for the distances involved in this book.

THE CYCLE RIDES

■ Children and safety

In the ten cycle rides in this book, we have taken great care to keep away from busy roads. Wherever possible, we have utilised traffic-free routes - the Hayling Billy Trail, the Meon Valley Cycle Trail are examples - but for most of the rides we have used the quietest and flattest country lanes that we can find. The traffic-free routes are suitable for children of almost any age, but with routes on public roads you need to think very carefully about whether your child has the necessary skills to cycle safely in traffic. Of one thing we can be certain, and that is that you and your family should always wear a helmet, as it offers a limited but significant amount of protection if you fall off and hit your head.

■ Your cycle

There are three basic types of bike available in the shops today that would be suitable for the rides in this book. Firstly, there is the touring bike, characterised by its drop handlebars and racks for carrying panniers. The mountain bike is rightly popular because of its ability to go anywhere, and it can now be bought with front and rear suspension, although this is not necessary for the rides in this book. Finally, there is the hybrid which looks like a mountain bike but has smaller diameter wheels and thinner tyres so you get the advantage of the robustness of a mountain bike with greater speed. All of the rides on surfaced roads in this book could be undertaken on all types, but the ones with significant off-road content would make a mountain or hybrid preferable. If you are not certain of the cycle that you wish to buy, try hiring one first. Then, when you have tried cycling again and find that it is enjoyable, go to a small shop that specialises in cycling and seek advice.

■ Clothing

On the upper half of the body it is best to follow the well-established layer principle, taking with you several layers of clothing rather than a single thick item, and peeling off or putting on as required. As far as wet weather protection is concerned, it is very advisable to listen to a weather forecast before you decide to go cycling and that way you can avoid the worst soaking. If you do cycle in the rain, no matter what you wear, you will find yourself getting clammy and probably wet anyway, due to the waterproof garment not "breathing" fast enough to rid the garment of perspiration, despite the claims of many manufacturers. If you take waterproofs, you will need to consider how you are going to carry them. A rucksack is feasible, but a better idea is a set of front or rear panniers, with the latter probably being the best. These avoid a sweaty back and have a low centre of gravity. If you think big and go for a large set of panniers, these could suffice for the whole family.

■ What to take

There is a minimal amount of kit that you need to take to stand you in good stead for most eventualities. The biggest worry is of course a puncture. To counter this you should ensure that you carry a pump with flexible connectors suitable for the range of tyre valves that you and your group may be using. We always carry both a puncture repair kit and a spare inner tube, on the grounds that if you are unable to repair a flat tyre your day out will be ruined. To accompany these, a set of three tyre levers are essential and an adjustable spanner with a capacity of up to about 25mm. In the heat of summer it is also important to remember to take sufficient drink to last you all day, so that you avoid becoming de-hydrated. You should also consider the best way to carry this guide book, or your map. You could use a handlebar mounted bag, which often has a clear pocket on top, or obtain a handlebar map carrier,

which are rare but very practical. Alternatively, you could use a walkers map carrier, slung over your back. This sounds impractical, but works quite well in practice. The minimal kit list for a wise family should therefore include:

• Waterproofs
• A pump with appropriate connectors
• A puncture repair kit
• A spare inner tube
• A set of tyre levers
• An adjustable spanner
• A small screwdriver
• A spray can of cycle oil
• Spare jumpers
• Gloves (for winter, spring and autumn)
• A lock
• A rag or some "wipes" to clean your hands after a repair
• Cycle bottles
• A map carrier or equivalent
• A small rucksack or pannier bag

Finally, the instructions given in the rides are recorded at specific distances. An inexpensive cycle computer would therefore be a useful aid.

RIGHTS OF WAY

Using the detailed instructions and high quality mapping in this guidebook, and the latest route information from our web site, you can relax in the knowledge that you are unlikely to run into any problems on your walks or rides. However, rights of way came into existence because at one time they served a social or economic need. They are one of our greatest assets and it is therefore important to have some knowledge of the law in respect of them. There are two main kinds of rights of way and these are footpaths and bridleways. Footpaths are for walkers only, and bridleways are for walkers, cyclists and riders on horseback. A third category know as a byway is very often an unsurfaced track that walkers, cyclists, riders and the very occasional vehicle usually have to share. All categories of rights of way are shown in this book in green on the walking maps, and in red on the cycling maps. Your rights when you are abroad in the countryside have been conveniently summarised by the Countryside Agency in the Countryside Access Charter below.

FREEDOM TO ROAM

The Countryside and Rights of Way Act has created a new legal right of access on foot to areas of open, uncultivated countryside in England and Wales. However, practical access will only be possible when conclusive maps have been produced in 3-4 years time.

USEFUL ADDRESSES

To report obstructions or other right of way problems:
• Public Rights of Way Officer, Countryside Services, Hampshire County Council, Basing House, Redbridge Lane, Basingstoke, RG24 7HB.
• Public Rights of Way Officer, Countryside Management Unit, West Sussex County Council, Chichester, West Sussex, PO19 1RH.
For more information on rambling:
• The Ramblers' Association, 2nd Floor, Camelford House, 87-90 Albert Embankment, London, SE1 7TW; E-mail: ramblers@london.ramblers.org.uk; Web: www.ramblers.org.uk
For more information on cycling:
• The Cyclists Touring Club (CTC), Cotterell House, 69 Meadrow, Godalming, Surrey, GU7 3HS; Web: www.ctc.org.uk
• Sustrans, 35 King Street, Bristol, BS1 4DZ; Web: www.sustrans.org.uk

The Countryside Access Charter

Your rights of way are:
• public footpaths - on foot only. Sometimes waymarked in yellow
• bridleways - on foot, horseback and pedal cycle. Sometimes waymarked in blue
• byways (usually old roads), most 'roads used as public paths' and of course, public roads - all traffic has the right of way
Use maps, signs and waymarks to check rights of way. Ordnance Survey Explorer and Landranger maps show most public rights of way

On rights of way you can:
• take a pram, pushchair or wheelchair if practicable
• take a dog (on a lead or under close control)
• take a short route round an illegal obstruction or remove it sufficiently to get past

You have a right to go for recreation to:
• public parks and open spaces on foot
• most commons near older towns and cities - on foot and sometimes on horseback
• private land where the owner has a formal agreement with the local authority

In addition you can use the following by local established custom or consent, but ask for advice if you are unsure:
• many areas of open country, such as moorland, fell and coastal areas, especially those in the care of the National Trust, and some commons
• some woods and forests, especially those owned by the Forestry Commission
• country parks and picnic sites
• most beaches
• canal towpaths
• some private paths and tracks
Consent sometimes extends to horse-riding and cycling

For your information:
• county councils and London Boroughs maintain and record rights of way and register commons
• obstructions, dangerous animals, harassment and misleading signs on rights of way are illegal and you should report them to the county council
• paths across fields can be ploughed but must normally be re-instated within two weeks
• landowners can require you to leave land to which you have no right of access
• motor vehicles are normally permitted only on roads, byways and some 'roads used as public paths'

INDEX